1982

The Making of the MICRO

A History of the Computer

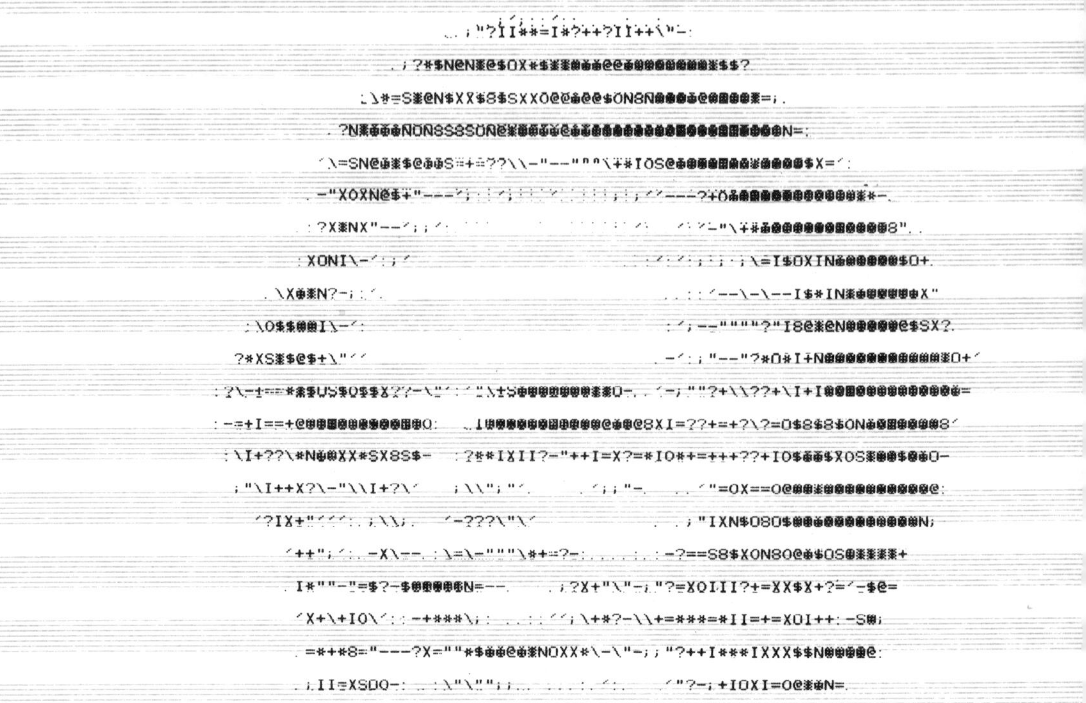

The Making of the MICRO

A History of the Computer

by Christopher Evans

Foreword by Tom Stonier

VAN NOSTRAND REINHOLD COMPANY
NEW YORK CINCINNATI TORONTO LONDON MELBOURNE

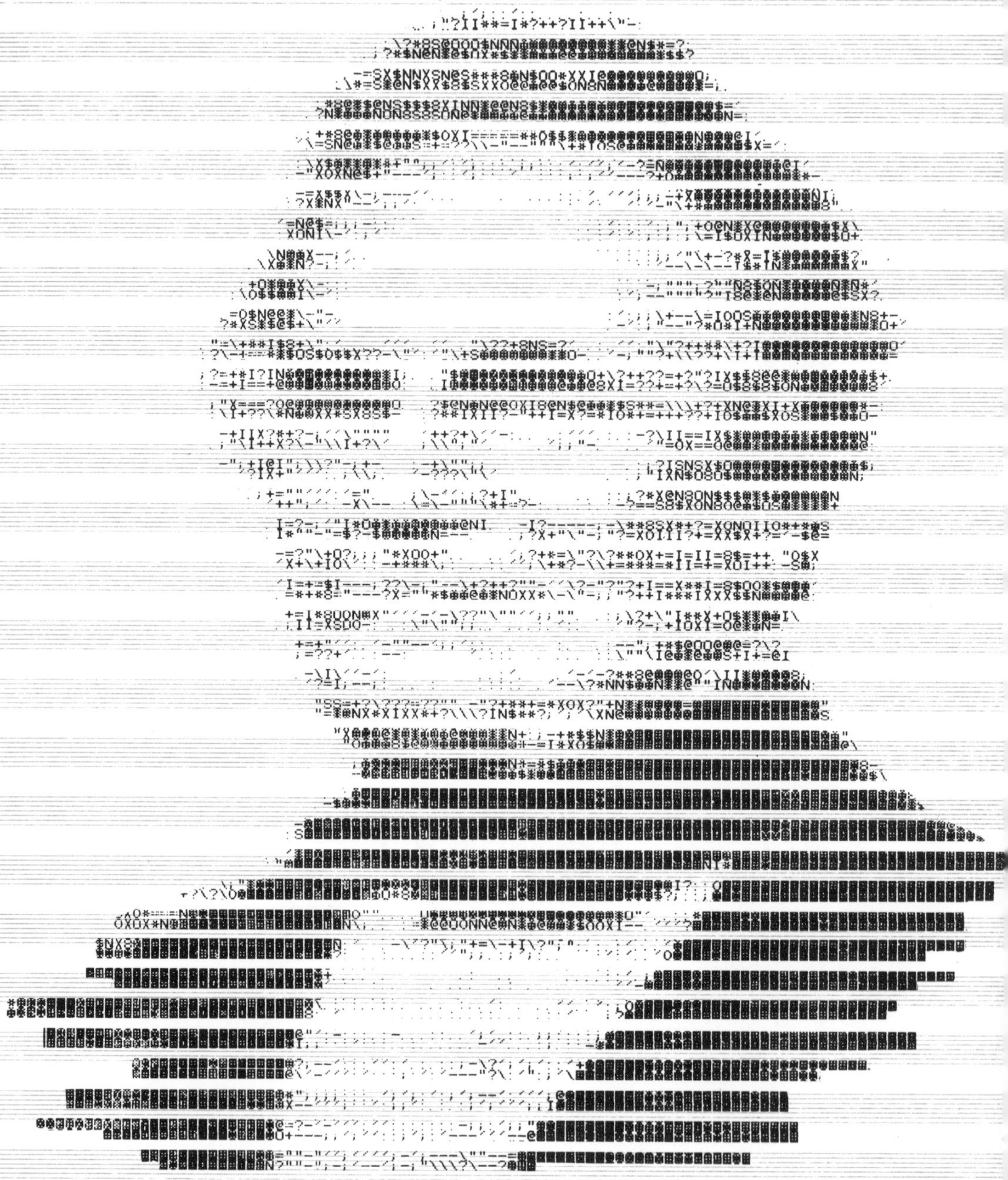

Contents

Copyright © 1981 by Harrow House Editions Ltd.

Library of Congress Catalog Card Number 81-4061

ISBN 0-442-22240-8

Printed in Belgium

Published by Van Nostrand Reinhold Company
A division of Litton Educational Publishing, Inc.
135 West 50th Street, New York, NY 10020, U.S.A.

16 15 14 13 12 11 10 9 8 7 6 5 4 3 2 1

Library of Congress Cataloging in Publication Data

Evans, Christopher Riche.
   The making of the micro.

"Some of this material has been published in abridged form in The micro millennium, Viking Penguin 1980".
   Bibliography: p.
   Includes index.
   1. Computers — History.   I. Title.
QA76.17.E92 1981   303.4'83   81-4061
ISBN 0-442-22240-8   AACR2

"One evening I was sitting in
the rooms of the Analytical
Society at Cambridge . . . with
a table of logarithms lying
open before me. Another
member coming into the room,
and seeing me half asleep
called out 'Well, Babbage, what
are you dreaming about?'
to which I replied, 'I am
thinking that all these tables
might be calculated by
machinery'."

Charles Babbage (1792–1871)

Foreword

A century or so ago, the Industrial Revolution was
having its full impact on Western society. Twenty years
ago, the Electronic Revolution was beginning to make
itself felt. Today, the Information Revolution is upon us.

The starting point of the Information Revolution is the
computer. Conceived by Charles Babbage (whose image
has been printed out by a computer on the opposite
page) and developed by many talented people including
Blaise Pascal, Otto Steiger, Konrad Zuse and Howard
Aiken, the computer is the product of numerous human
brains which over centuries have analysed, calculated
and toiled to perfect a machine that could extend our
mental faculties, just as the Industrial Revolution
extended our physical and mechanical faculties.

What will this new information do? What will be the
impact of the Information Revolution? Massive dole
queues? Electronic warfare? Big Brother keeping track of
everything with his computers?

Or will we begin to live richer, more satisfying lives
as the robots working automated farms and factories
provide us with all our material needs, leaving us to care
for each other and enjoy life?

Which of these two roads we take will depend on how
sophisticated we become. The greatest bulwark against
the slide into an electronic "Dark Age" is an informed
public opinion. An educated citizenry learns to exploit
new technology. An ignorant one becomes its victim.

Chris Evans understood well the future rushing upon
us: an exhilarating, fascinating future full of promise.
This book is his story of how the mighty micro came to be.

Tom Stonier, 1980

INTRODUCTION
1984 or Brave New World?

In 1949, when I was leaving school, my reading was almost entirely devoted to science fiction, then something of a minority interest and generally dismissed by most people as juvenile and disreputable. This troubled me not the slightest, as the message that sprang from the pages of the imported pulp magazines was one so exciting and thrilling that the opinion of others was of no consequence. The message was that the world I lived in was about to enter a period of great, perhaps convulsive, change. The future was coming up fast and it was going to be so staggeringly different from the present that all social, political, economic, technological and even psychological values would have to be changed. Mind you, it wasn't too clear from the magazines exactly which of the widely differing pictures of the future were the most likely to come about. The only thing one could be sure of was that things were going to change, and they were going to change fast.

That was the message from the pulp magazines. But there were other sources of inspiration, and of all the reading material I devoured at the time two books in particular really made an impression on me. Perhaps this was because they presented such contradictory views of the future, one offering something that seemed as close to hell on earth as could be imagined, the other an almost Utopian vision—perhaps one would say a Utopia with a quirk. They were George Orwell's *1984*, and Aldous Huxley's *Brave New World*.

In the summer of 1949 I read them both over and over again, trying to decide which of the two futures they depicted was the more likely to come true. There was no doubt which was the *preferred* future, but which was the more likely? At the time Orwell's gloomy vision seemed to be not only more probable but also more imminent, for England seemed an incredibly gloomy place. Food was scarce and awful, clothing was drab, buses and trains were overcrowded and bomb sites were all over the place. There was a feeling that everything was slowly getting slightly worse and it wasn't at all difficult to imagine the London of 1949 sliding gently into the kind of London portrayed in *1984*, and quite possibly decades ahead of time.

The other book, *Brave New World*, was different in tone and content. It was set much further ahead in time—the year 2500 or thereabouts—and it seemed to depict an almost totally *un*likely kind of future. The colossal affluence of the society, the easy nonchalance with which its citizens accepted their disease-free, dirt-free, anxiety-free lives, and the internal complacency and self-sufficiency of the society itself were virtually unbelievable. And yet, on re-reading both books thirty years later, one is immediately impressed by the fact that whereas it now seems to be rather unlikely that the Orwellian vision of *1984* will ever be realized, let alone by its target date, the weird Utopia that Huxley portrayed may be much closer than we think. Some of his predictions, tied up though they are in allegory and satire, have been almost uncannily successful, particularly when one recalls that he was writing before the motor car had risen to be the crucial status symbol of the twentieth century, before the great established religions had tumbled into trendiness and irrelevance, before the collapse of sexual taboos and the virtual emancipation of women, before the word—or even concept—of cloning had drifted into usage, before the rise of a huge and affluent middle class, increasingly preoccupied with games, leisure activities and banal TV, before the widespread use of tranquillisers. . . . All of this he stunningly foretold.

This reversal of probability in two widely differing views of the future occurred over a short space of time and should serve as a timely warning about the dangers of making sweeping statements about the future. Furthermore it's a warning that I, as a science fiction fan and one well versed in the mercurial powers of prediction, should heed above all. But I believe that a future is imminent whose progress can be plotted with some degree of precision. It is a future which will involve, *must* involve, a transformation of world society at all kinds of levels, which, while taking place slowly at first, will gather pace with sudden force. It's a future which is largely moulded by a single, startling development in technology whose first real impact is now beginning to be felt. The piece of technology I am talking about is, of course, the computer, and it is significant that the word doesn't appear once in either *1984* or *Brave New World*.

Threats or promises that the world is about to be transformed are by no means uncommon, and the human race as a whole pays little attention to them. Sometimes individuals or small groups respond in deadly earnest to particular predictions. One minority religious sect, for example, recently sold all their belongings and camped out on the top of a mountain to await the flying saucer which was scheduled to rescue them before a tidal wave engulfed the earth. On another occasion numerous people left their homes in San Francisco at the time and date predicted by the Victorian seer Edgar Cayce for the next devastating earthquake in that city. Thousands have been surprised or disappointed by the failure of these and other events to materialize.

Indeed, events that are potent and radical enough to exert a force significantly large to overcome the huge social, economic and psychological inertia of the earth's population tend to be extremely rare—even global wars affect only a small percentage of the population to any significant degree, and the same is true of famines, floods, earthquakes, the rise and fall of dynasties and just about anything else that one can think of. Furthermore, earth-shaking events seem, by their nature, to be rarely predictable with any degree of accuracy, and the things that one feels most confident about have a funny way of evaporating into thin air. But there have been global trends which *have* had enduring, if rather long-term, significance. The discovery of navigational techniques is one example of many, as was the inventing of printing. More recent, more far reaching even, and more rapid in the speed with which it unleashed its effects was the Industrial Revolution.

The Industrial Revolution, as everyone knows, changed the face first of Britain and then of a large part of the rest of the world. Hills and valleys where sheep and cows had grazed for thousands of years were dug open and blackened in the quest for coal. Sleepy country towns which had barely grown in size since the time of the Roman domination of the country ballooned into ugly manufacturing cities. At the same time the new industries sucked in migrant workers from all parts of the country, bringing about a major redistribution of population with its inevitably unsettling social and cultural effects. Communications networks improved dramatically, dragging in their wake even more rapid movement and population shift. But most important of all, the coming of the new industries brought about a great increase in national affluence, unevenly distributed to be sure, but spreading down from the coal owners and steel magnates at the top to the hard-grinding labourers at the bottom. In less than a century England was transformed from a predominantly agricultural community into a bustling industrial nation with an expanding, increasingly wealthy population. And hand in hand with this came the inevitable political changes as power began to devolve from the hands of monarchs and autocrats, first to the industrialists, later to their managers and finally—a process which is still only partially completed—to the working people themselves.

There are four important features of the Industrial Revolution which need to be identified and considered, for they are also extremely significant for the next great turning point which mankind is rapidly approaching—the Computer Revolution. The first of these concerns the wide scale and scope of change—the Industrial Revolution brought immense shifts in all aspects of human society, affecting the individual, his family, his neighbours, his domestic and working environment, his clothes, his food, his leisure time, his political and religious ideals, his education, his social attitudes, his life span, even the manner of his birth and death. The second highly significant feature is that these changes took place with great rapidity, re-moulding the face of man and his society in less than a hundred years. Thirdly, once the process of the Revolution was fully under way, its dynamism grew remorselessly and no power, no man or combination of men could set it back against its course. Finally—and perhaps the most interesting of the four points—hardly anyone, and certainly no one who could do anything about it, foresaw its momentous coming, nor envisaged its spectacular progress once it had got under way. Only the gallantly misguided Luddites, who feared *decreased* affluence from the coming of the machines, seemed to have any glimmering of insight into what was about to happen.

The Computer Revolution is the natural and proper successor to the Industrial Revolution, the significant difference being that we now move from the amplification and replacement of the power of muscles to the amplification and ultimate emancipation of the power of the brain. As with the Industrial Revolution it will have overwhelming and comprehensive impact, affecting every human being on earth in every aspect of his or her life. Again, paralleling its predecessor, the Computer Revolution will run at a gallop, though its time course will be shorter and its force may well be spent not in 150 years, but in twenty-five. Thirdly—again note the parallel—the revolutionary process once under way will be unstoppable. Finally (and here for the first time we have an essential point of difference), whereas the Victorian machine age began, surged into motion and, indeed, almost ran its course before most people were aware of what had happened, we stand today with a knowledge of the past, and, more important, with an understanding, in general, of what is likely to happen in the future.

The history of computers is a fascinating area largely unknown to most people. A knowledge of their evolution from their earliest beginnings to the present day and the social and economic pressures which brought them into being will help the reader to understand the nature of their inevitable evolution in the future. The history of computers also introduces some of the remarkable human beings who worked on them and their forerunners, the people who have given us our powerful new servants.

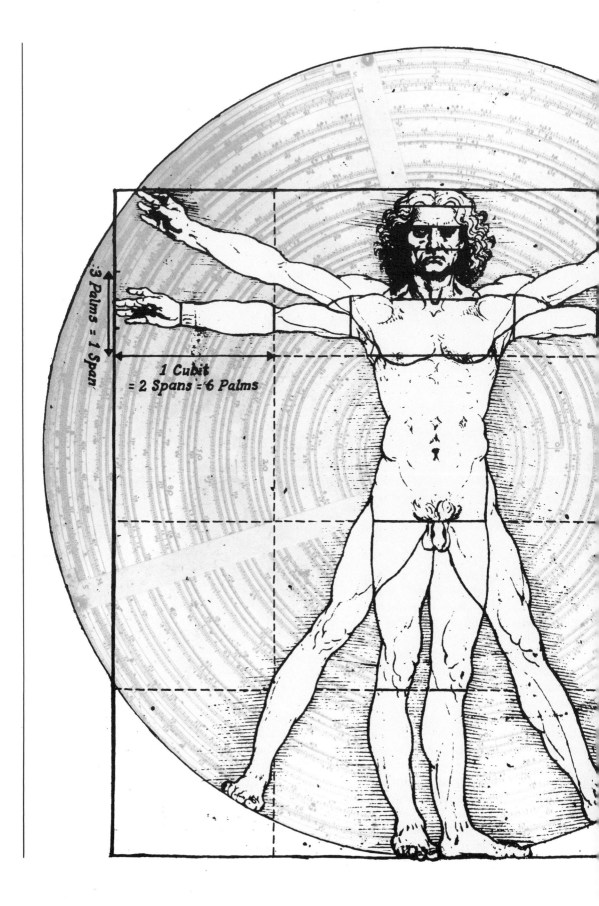

Machines that Count

In one sense, computers have had a brief history—not much more than thirty-five years. In another sense their use stretches back in time to the first occasion when Man picked up a few small stones or scratched marks in the earth as a kind of record or memory aid. What he was doing in each case was using a physical unit or sets of units to represent numbers or quantities, and the essence of computers is in fact just this: a number or a quantity can be represented by a physical thing, whether it is a pebble, a bead on a wire, a mark on a bit of paper, a mechanical gear wheel, an electrical relay, a vacuum tube or a sub-microscopic area of magnetized material. Once numbers can be expressed in this physical way, it becomes possible to manipulate them or change their state, and by doing so cause them to represent different numbers or quantities. This in turn means that, in principle at any rate, it should be possible to construct a machine to perform these manipulations and thus act as an automatic calculator.

The word calculator has crept in here, you will notice, while earlier on I have used the word computer. There is a difference between the meanings of the two words which we will go into in a bit more detail later, but for the moment we'll treat the two as equal.

The important point to grasp here—and it is really all one needs to know about the physical make-up of computers in order to understand and follow the rest of this book—is that while numbers are abstract in one sense, they are really all expressible as physical units or chunks and that provided one chooses the right kind of physical chunk to express them in, it becomes possible to calculate with them and to store them over time.

A crude and simple example of storage and calculation is the milometer on a motor car with which almost every reader, no matter how innumerate, will be familiar. Here the mileage covered by the car is expressed by a row of numbers in a window, and these numbers merely reflect the positions of a set of interlocking cogs behind them. These cogs (each of which has ten teeth) record tenths of miles, miles, tens of miles, hundreds of miles and so on. No doubt this will all seem maddeningly obvious to anyone who knows anything about motor cars, but we will press on at this simple level for a while longer: as the road wheels of the car turn they also cause the first of the cog-wheels to turn, displaying a sequence of "tenths-of-mile" units in its window, and a complete revolution is made each time

Below: Tally sticks were used as receipts before decimal notation became accepted. The different shapes of the notches represent different units of currency. Tally sticks were used less and less until they were ceremonially burned in 1834.

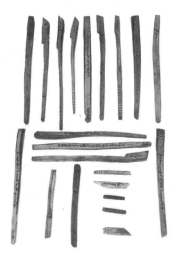

Above: The earliest calculating machines added numbers in exactly the same way as a milometer. The first of the cog wheels is activated by the wheels of the car and tenths-of-mile units are displayed. Each time a mile is covered, the cog wheels have made a complete revolution and at this point a small lever knocks one of the teeth on the mile-recording cog, raising the miles shown by one. After ten such blows from the mile-recording cog, it delivers a tap to the 10-mile cog and so on. This mechanism is exactly the same as the tens-carry mechanism used in the earliest calculators.

a mile has been covered. On the completion of each revolution a small lever on the side of the first cog hits one of the teeth on the mile-recording cog next to it, causing it to turn through a tenth of a revolution and the appropriate "mile" number is displayed in the window. After ten such blows it too has revolved completely and now delivers a tap to the ten-mile cog next to it, and so on. The lever which passes the message from one cog to another is, of course, the equivalent of the "carry" in paper-and-pencil arithmetic.

Now, at an exceptionally crude level, what we have been describing is the operation of a very simple mechanical calculator which has (a) counted distances in decimal units, (b) added tenths of miles to make miles, miles to make tens of miles and so on, and (c) displayed its "answer" in a way that a human can read. Strictly speaking this is a mechanical "adder"—it can't multiply or divide, though it might be able to "subtract" if you drove the car in reverse. In addition to these simple calculations, the milometer "remembers" the mileage the car has covered and displays this ready for the motorist when he starts off on his next trip.

It would be wrong to give the impression that these kinds of metallic clankings and wheel turnings represent the basic mode of operation of modern computers; as we shall see, totally different methods of representing and calculating numbers are now employed and the computation can be done at stupendous—there is no other word for it—speeds. But the example of the milometer will do to introduce the central concept of machines counting numbers and doing something with them, and that, as I have said, is all that has to be grasped.

Clearly there were calculators of one kind or another before the invention of the car milometer, and the most commonly cited example of a primitive device which has had a long run for its money—it has been around for about five thousand years—is the abacus. The abacus is a collection of beads on a series of rods or wires, and the position of the beads in relation to one or other end of the frame denotes their number. Different levels of the frame are used to denote different parts of the sum to be calculated, and computation is performed by moving the beads back and forth according to a set of rules. People get to be very nimble at operating the abacus, incidentally, and once in a while someone is sufficiently impressed by the speed with which the operators perform to be inspired to match them against a human using an electrical calculator. Shortly after the last war a famous duel of this kind took place in Tokyo, when a clerk named Matsuzake from one of the Japanese Ministries, using only his abacus, took on a

Private First Class Tom Wood of the US Army using what was, at the time, the very latest in electro-mechanical desk calculators. Mr Matsuzake whipped Private Wood in overall performance to the audience's great delight, for everyone likes to see machines with intellectual pretensions being made to look foolish.

Alas, there would be no hope of the abacus beating even today's cheapest pocket calculators. Its use has only recently died out in Japan, and once in a while in a country store you will still see the owner totting up the bill with his frame of beads, the last of a long, long line of users. But there is one important point to make about the abacus before we pass on: while it employs the fundamental strategy of the calculator/computer by representing numbers or quantities as physical objects or states, it has to have a human to manipulate the beads, and it needs, therefore, a source of power and something to direct its sequence of operation. It may seem blindingly obvious that the abacus could hardly be expected to move under its own power and decide *for itself* what calculations to perform and when and how to carry them out, but this represents a fairly substantial difference between the abacus and the first true calculating machines.

Part of the spur to develop devices like the abacus—there were several different types of them being used all over the world at one time—was the enormous difficulty people experienced in doing pencil-and-paper calculations with the common systems of notation then in use. Try to imagine a method of multiplying the following Roman numerals:

CCXXXII times XLVIII

The problem is even worse in ancient Chinese notation, but when translated into the far simpler and more efficient

Below: The abacus could in the hands of a skilled operator out-perform calculators until the electronic age, and they are still used in the Far East today.

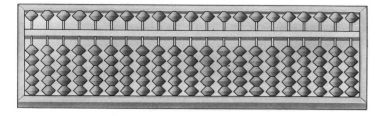

1 9 6 3 7

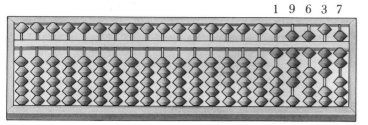

Left: Each column represents one digit. The abacus on the left is set in the zero position. Digits from 1 to 4 are shown by moving beads below the divider bar upwards. 5 is shown by moving the bead at the top downwards. Digits between 6 and 9 are shown by moving the 5 bead downwards and from 1 to 4 of the bottom beads upwards. For example, 1 is shown by a single lower bead being pushed upwards to the divider bar; to show 9 four of the lower beads are pushed up to the divider bar and the 5 bead down to the bar.

Arabic numerals, the sum becomes 232 times 48 and the whole thing takes on a different complexion. This isn't simply because we are more familiar with Arabic numerals; they actually are far easier to perform written calculations with, and those societies which adopted them when they first came on the scene—including all Europe west of Russia—not only freed themselves from having to use the abacus for every non-trivial calculation but also opened the way for their scholars to delve into levels of mathematics beyond the scope of those stuck with more primitive notational methods. Among those who did not adopt Arabic notation were the Greeks, whose vigorous thrust in philosophy was poorly matched—even to some extent handicapped—by their weakly developed mathematics.

But even Arabic numbers don't make for effortless calculating. As medieval societies became more complex and dependent upon extensive economic exchanges, so the amount of routine calculations that had to be churned out grew and grew. Most of this was sheer drudgery and too much for the average individual, who, by the way, was more or less totally innumerate. Even educated people were not taught rudimentary mathematics in their basic schooling—a surprising fact which one discovers if one browses through the literature of the time. Even as late as the seventeenth century people could hold high positions in government and commerce and yet remain more or less clueless when it came to multiplication and division. In his diary, for example, we find Samuel Pepys, who was a senior civil servant in charge of the administration of the Royal Navy, moaning and groaning about having to sit up halfway through the night swotting his eight times table. Some businessmen and accountants attempted to master huge sets of tables—up to 24 times 24 for example—but few were able to persist with this nightmare discipline. A better solution, if one could afford it, was to hire a professional "mathematician" to do the routine number-crunching, but even these people found it impossible to work for more than an hour or so at a stretch without fatigue and error creeping in. It is not surprising, therefore, that the invention of the slide-rule in the latter half of the seventeenth century was greeted with shouts of joy.

The slide-rule, which had an active life of over three centuries as a mathematician's tool before it was suddenly and ingloriously consigned to the scrap-heap in the mid-1970s by the appearance of pocket calculators, was an invention which sprang naturally out of the discovery of logarithms by John Napier.

Napier was a Scotsman; he was extremely active in the Church politics of the time and was a particularly cranky anti-Catholic. He also fancied himself as an inventor of military weapons and designed quite a few, including a metal-covered chariot with slots to shoot out of—I suppose one might call it a forerunner of the tank—and a weird assembly of mirrors and lenses by which he hoped to focus the sun to frizzle up enemies at a distance. None of these came to much as it happens, but he did discover logarithms and for that alone he can be said to have paid his dues.

Logarithms, as most schoolchildren know—or at least used to know, because logarithms as calculation aids are also being whisked away on the winds of history—are tables of numbers which greatly simplify routine multiplication and division. The principle is based on the fact that for every positive number, as Napier discovered, there exists another number (called its logarithm) and that the relationship between them is such that the multiplication of any two numbers is achieved by *adding* their logarithms. Division is achieved by *subtracting* their logarithms. The drawback to the method is that you have to convert the numbers to their appropriate logs by looking them up in a table, and after you have done the sum, reconvert the added or subtracted total to "real" numbers by looking it up in an "anti-log" table. The tables are a bit of a bore, but the whole process is far simpler than routine multiplication and division, particularly when strings of calculations are involved. Now, the concept of logarithms is a very important one in mathematical theory, but there is another aspect of them that soon attracted attention. Smart people thinking about the fact that logarithms are, as it were, compressed versions of their original numbers, realized that these could easily be converted into lengths on a scale or ruler, and multiplication and division could be achieved by simply adding or subtracting the two lengths on the scale. From this point the concept of the slide-rule more or less springs to mind. The first of these marvellously useful devices was built by an English clergyman named Oughtred, and an improved commercial version appeared in 1621.

Curiously, Napier himself doesn't seem to have thought of the slide-rule, but he did get another very clever idea, which was to lay out multiplication tables on the faces of a set of four-sided segmented rods; you turned the appropriate wooden rods (there was one for each of the ten digits) and added or subtracted whatever numbers came up on the exposed faces. The set of wooden rods was mounted nicely in a wooden box with instructions on the lid and they became known as Napier's Bones. Some people like to think of them as the first calculating machine, but that is a misunderstanding of their function. The "Bones" were only a restricted set of multiplication tables made available

	0	1	2	3	4	5	6	7	8	9	1 2 3	4 5 6	7 8 9
10	0000	0043	0086	0128	0170	0212	0253	0294	0334	0374	4 8 12	17 21 25	29 33 37
11	0414	0453	0492	0531	0569	0607	0645	0682	0719	0755	4 8 11	15 19 23	26 30 34
12	0792	0828	0864	0899	0934	0969	1004	1038	1072	1106	3 7 10	14 17 21	24 28 31
13	1139	1173	1206	1239	1271	1303	1335	1367	1399	1430	3 6 10	13 16 19	23 26 29
14	1461	1492	1523	1553	1584	1614	1644	1673	1703	1732	3 6 9	12 15 18	21 24 27
15	1761	1790	1818	1847	1875	1903	1931	1959	1987	2014	3 6 8	11 14 17	20 22 25
16	2041	2068	2095	2122	2148	2175	2201	2227	2253	2279	3 5 8	11 13 16	18 21 24
17	2304	2330	2355	2380	2405	2430	2455	2480	2504	2529	2 5 7	10 12 15	17 20 22
18	2553	2577	2601	2625	2648	2672	2695	2718	2742	2765	2 5 7	9 12 14	16 19 21
19	2788	2810	2833	2856	2878	2900	2923	2945	2967	2989	2 4 7	9 11 13	16 18 20
20	3010	3032	3054	3075	3096	3118	3139	3160	3181	3201	2 4 6	8 11 13	15 17 19

Above: **John Napier (1550–1617)**, Scottish mathematician and theologian is remembered chiefly for introducing logarithms to mathematics. After travelling on the Continent Napier began his mathematical work in 1573 by attempting to systematize algebraic knowledge. His desire to abolish the drudgery of calculation resulted in the invention of logarithms in 1614 and in the simple mechanical device known as Napier's Bones in 1617, which in turn led to the invention of the slide-rule by William Oughtred. Napier was also interested in astrology and divination.

Above: Logarithms are one of the many developments in the history of computation which have sought to simplify the processes of multiplication and division. The principle is based on the fact that for every number there exists another number, called its logarithm. The relationship between the number and its logarithm is such that the multiplication of any two numbers is achieved by adding their logarithms. Division is achieved by subtracting the logarithms. In the example the multiplication sum 1.083×1.748 is being performed. The first step is to discover the logarithms by reference to a set of tables. They come to 0.0346 and 0.2425. These numbers are added together, and the result is decoded to produce a real number of 1.893, which is the answer to the sum. In practice, logarithms are normally decoded by reference to a separate set of tables known as anti-logs.

Right: Napier's Bones were another aid to multiplication, and consisted of a set of nine square-section rods divided into segments (examples are shown bottom right). The rods were numbered in arithmetic sequence enabling multiplications to be performed by adding together the figures shown. In the example (right), the number 1,572 is multiplied by the digits 4 and 9. First, the appropriate rods for 1,572 are set up in the right of the tray. Then, using the index column on the extreme left, results for the multipliers 4 and 9 are read off. Each digit of the answer is arrived at by adding together the figures between the diagonal lines.

in a novel and accessible form, and all the calculations themselves had to be done by the user. The types of calculations you could perform with them were really extremely trivial—the kind of thing anyone can do in their heads now—and the fact that they were invented at all and sold in quite large numbers is a testimony to the poor state of mathematical education of the time. Even then they were only popular for a few decades, partly because they were rather expensive to make, but mainly because most people found log tables and slide-rules to be far more useful.

The first true machine capable of performing arithmetical functions followed on about a quarter of a century after

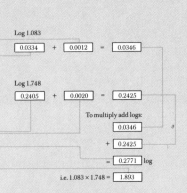

Log 1.083

0.0334	+	0.0012	=	0.0346

Log 1.748

0.2405	+	0.0020	=	0.2425

To multiply add logs:

$$0.0346$$
$$+\ 0.2425$$
$$=\ 0.2771 \text{ log}$$

i.e. $1.083 \times 1.748 = 1.893$

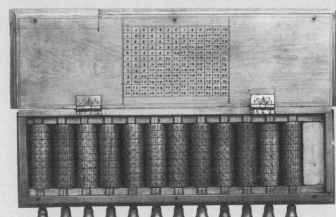

Right: This is an adaptation of Napier's Bones, with 12 cylindrical rods permanently mounted in a case. An addition table is pasted to the lid.

$1572 \times 4 = 6288$

$1572 \times 9 = 14{,}148$

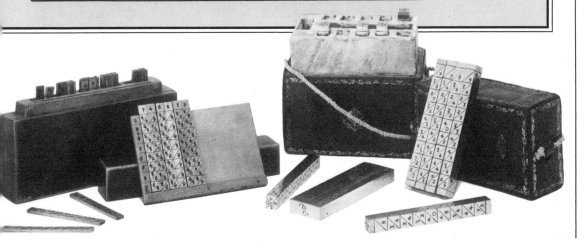

logarithms and it made no use of Napier's discovery whatsoever. Its principle of operation was crude, and all it really did was add, but it *was* mechanical and it was the first of its kind in the world. Its inventor was another vigorous intellectual, capable of turning his mind to more or less anything that intrigued him and he was miles ahead of most of his contemporaries in terms of vision and imagination. His name was Blaise Pascal.

Pascal was a funny looking child, slightly humpbacked and given to fits. His oddness was so marked that his family were confident that someone had cast a spell on him at birth, and a big effort was made to track down whoever was responsible. In due course a woman was found who admitted that she had cursed him because she had a grudge

William Oughtred
(1575–1660), English mathematician and clergyman, was educated at Eton and Cambridge. He became vicar of Salford in 1604, and rector of Albury, Surrey, in 1631. Oughtred was a keen amateur mathematician who is credited with inventing the earliest form of slide-rule—a device which Samuel Pepys (1633–1703) pronounced "very pretty for all questions of arithmetic". Oughtred published *Clavis Mathematica* (1631), in which he introduced the symbol × for multiplication. He also introduced the terms sine, cosine and tangent for common trigonometrical ratios.

Below: Like logarithms and Napier's bones, the slide-rule was invented to make multiplication and division easier. A series of different scales are engraved on the fixed part of the rule, and the moving part can then be manipulated to perform a variety of calculations. In the first example shown, 3 is being multiplied by 6. The transparent guide is aligned with the 6 on the scale marked D, and the slide is then moved to the right so that the red 3 engraved on it is similarly aligned. The answer 18 is then read off from the place indicated by the left-hand end of the slide. In the second example, 20 is being divided by 4. The guide is aligned with the 2 on scale D, and the slide moved to the right until the 4 engraved on it is also in line. The result 5 is read off from the place indicated by the right-hand end of the slide. The same actions would be performed if the dividend were 2 or 200; the result would then be interpreted as 0.5 or 50 respectively.

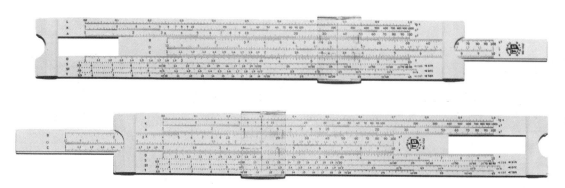

against his father, who had been giving her a hard time in his capacity as a tax collector. She agreed to remove the spell but told the Pascals that they would have to sacrifice a horse first. After pondering the difficulties of this, they went back and asked if a smaller animal might not do. She agreed to compromise, and after selecting a cat, flung it out of a third storey window, whereupon everyone agreed that the spell had been removed. Blaise himself never got to look any less peculiar unfortunately, and went through life with all kinds of afflictions, including a painful and debilitating form of neural disease. But he did blossom rapidly into a mathematical prodigy and before he was in his teens he was working on a completely novel approach to conical geometry and was serving on a committee to establish the optimum method of determining longitudes. He also spotted a not-very-obvious error in one of Descartes' mathematical arguments. This thoroughly irritated Descartes, and for years he followed the rocketing progress of Pascal with spiteful envy, reviewing his works dismissively.

Pascal was probably moved by the sight of his father labouring away into the night on the financial calculations which were his bread and butter to generate the design for his mechanical adder. Today it looks pretty unimpressive, a set of interlocking cogs and wheels on various axles, but it *was* the world's first calculating machine. You set up the numbers you wished to add by literally dialling them into the machine, and the act of dialling caused the cogs and wheels inside to rotate appropriately. When you'd finished dialling in the last number, the result—which of course merely expressed the new positions of the wheels inside— was displayed in a little window. You could easily build one today with a Meccano set, but at the time no one had even conceived of such a thing. Pascal and his father rushed around all over the place demonstrating it to royalty, politicians, scientists and businessmen. It was called, appropriately, the Pascaline, and everyone was suitably amazed. A machine that could add! It could subtract too, incidentally, though you had to make an adjustment inside to cause the machine to "count backwards". With a bit more effort it could multiply by a series of repeated additions, or divide by repeated subtractions, which is the way that most mechanical calculators operated until quite recently.

The cleverness of the device lay in the fact that Pascal had realized how a machine could tackle the task of "carrying", a problem which had to be solved if one was going to compute numbers larger than ten, and the principle is the same as that used in the milometer: when one ten-cogged wheel has moved its full circle it triggers a second ten-cogged

Pierre de Fermat (1601–65), French jurist and mathematician, partly anticipated Leibniz' work on differential calculus and collaborated with Pascal (1623–62) on the fundamentals of probability theory. Fermat was a purely amateur mathematician who contributed to the theory of numbers and partly anticipated Descartes' (1596–1650) analytical geometry and the differential calculus of Leibniz (1646–1716). His "last theorem" still lacks a proof, although Fermat claimed to have found one adding in an annotation that "this margin is too small to contain it".

wheel to move one tenth of *its* circumference and so on. The Pascaline was in essence foolproof and incapable of error, and as it would undoubtedly take the drudgery out of much routine calculation, Blaise and his papa can be forgiven for assuming that they would make their fortunes out of it. Financial resources were pooled and a number of units were constructed and marketed, but few, if any, buyers were found. The reasons were simple and are often encountered today in computerizing some modern business organizations. No one doubted that the Pascaline would work: indeed you didn't have to have a lot of brains to be able to understand its principles and appreciate exactly how and why it worked as well as it did. More to the point was the fact that the clerks and accountants employed by the potential customers of the machines were unashamedly afraid that if many of the things were purchased they would be out of a job. They didn't get around, like their indirect descendants, the Luddites, to smashing up any Pascalines,

Left: **Blaise Pascal (1623–62)**, French mathematician, physicist, religious philosopher, writer and scientific inventor, was educated by his father, Etienne, presiding judge of the tax court at Clermont-Ferrand and a respected mathematician. At the age of 11, Blaise Pascal had calculated for himself the first 23 propositions of Euclid, and at 16 he published a paper on solid geometry. Between 1642 and

1644 Pascal invented the Pascaline to help his father in tax computations.

Below: The Pascaline was the first significant calculating machine. The numbers to be added together are dialled in via the row of numbered wheels at the bottom, and the result shows in the square windows at the top. The machine was also capable of subtraction.

but they did put open pressure on their bosses. This attitude is interesting as a precursor of much of the present resistance to automation and computerization, but it is not actually the most important factor.

It is a basic tenet of capitalism that profitability is the first thing to strive for in business, and if the businessmen of the time felt that Pascal's invention would save them significant sums of money they would probably have bought them in vast numbers and cheerfully sacked their armies of clerks and accountants. But a Pascaline was rather an expensive instrument to buy and, while its running costs were almost zero, its repair and maintenance would not be cheap. Against this, the clerks and accountants were extremely cheap and, of course, they did the whole job while the mechanical adder only did a part of it. The sole justification for a Pascaline would be to make life a bit easier for the drudge accountants, and why waste money on them? So the brilliant invention was a flop economically, if not scientifically. Until very recently you could buy a tiny mechanical pocket calculator which was nothing more than a miniaturized version of Pascal's original design. I have seen it advertised alongside rupture appliances, new kinds of garden fertilizer and cheap digital watches in newspapers all over the world, so in the end the Pascaline made some money for somebody. Pascal himself went on to invent the hydraulic press, the barometer, the wheelbarrow and one or two other useful things, and he also co-operated with Fermat on developing the fundamentals of probability theory before he died at the early age of thirty-nine.

Businessmen may have rejected the world's first mechanical calculator, but men of science were less able to do so. One of the first people to inspect one in operation and have a really good think about it was another polymath genius, Gottfried Leibniz. Born in Saxony in 1646, just after Pascal had put together the first of his adders, Leibniz was another child prodigy, who, after the fashion of his kind, was writing Greek and Latin verse by the time he was ten and had moved on to the principles of formal logic in his early teens. By the time he was eighteen he had written a stunning philosophical dissertation on the question of whether things actually exist as individual entities or only in terms of their perceived qualities. Most people get through life without even being aware of this problem, let alone getting to grips with it, but Leibniz had settled it all in his mind while he was still very young. Next he moved on to attempt to develop a mathematics of truth and reason which would offer a universal language capable of solving all philosophical arguments. This requires there to be only a limited number

Above: **René Descartes** (**1596–1650**), French philosopher and mathematician, founded analytical geometry and discovered the laws of geometric optics. Descartes was responsible for the Cartesian system, a method of reasoning which established the ideal of mathematical certitude. His prolific output, both in books and correspondence, led to his being acclaimed as a philosopher, and he may be regarded as the "father of modern philosophy".
Much travelled in Europe, Descartes eventually agreed to instruct Queen Christina of Sweden in philosophy. Lessons were scheduled for 5 a.m. each morning and this, coupled with the unaccustomed climate, caused Descartes a fatal attack of pneumonia.

of "truths" or "facts" in the world, all of which can be specified rather precisely. In this ambitious venture Leibniz leant heavily on the works of a thirteenth-century priest, Ramon Llull, whose exercises in symbolic logic lie partly in the realm of genius and partly in the netherland of crankiness. Like many mathematicians and logicians of the time, Llull felt that one ought, by the totally pure (i.e. non-evil) science of mathematics, to be able to prove the existence of God. Leibniz eventually came to discard most Llullian ideas, but unfortunately kept the bit about proving the existence of God—an obsession which was to have odd consequences, as we shall see.

Leibniz quickly saw that the Pascaline's great weakness was that the tasks of multiplication and division were only tackled in a most laborious fashion, and that any mechanical calculator worth constructing and selling would have to work on a different principle. He solved the problem by introducing a new kind of multiplier wheel, which was

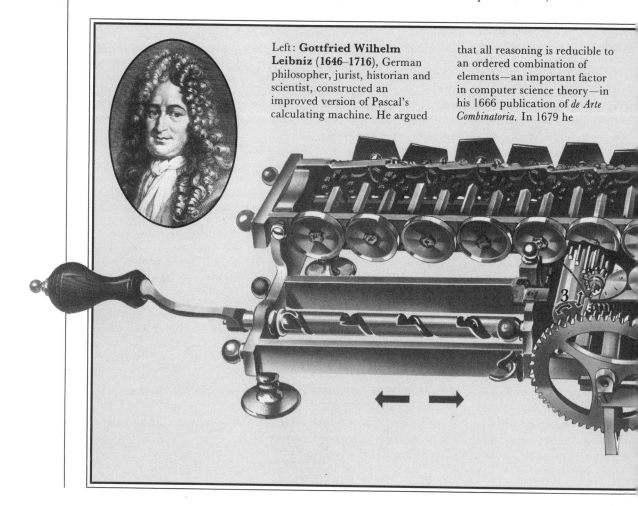

Left: **Gottfried Wilhelm Leibniz (1646–1716)**, German philosopher, jurist, historian and scientist, constructed an improved version of Pascal's calculating machine. He argued that all reasoning is reducible to an ordered combination of elements—an important factor in computer science theory—in his 1666 publication of *de Arte Combinatoria*. In 1679 he

stepped with nine teeth of different lengths. For anyone fascinated with these kinds of engineering details there are plenty of good accounts of its operation, and a working model is on display in the Science Museum, London. This stepped wheel made the important advance of making multiplication a distinct operation. It was a brilliant idea and it really worked, and the chances are that if you pull apart one of the electro-mechanical calculators of the 1960s, now gathering dust in the corners of many schools and research laboratories, you will see how his invention survived three hundred years. There's no doubt that it markedly speeded up all kinds of routine calculation, unlike Pascal's which merely made them a bit easier, and if he had pushed ahead with its manufacture it might well have sold in large numbers. But by then he was bored with the project and moved on to other things. Included among the "other things" were developing the notation of differential calculus, attempting to reunite the Protestant and Catholic Churches

Ramon Llull (c. 1235–1315), known as Doctor Illuminatus, was a Catalan writer, philosopher and lay missionary. After spending a dissolute youth as a soldier, he was converted to a religious life in about 1266, devoting himself to missionary work and the teaching of foreign languages. His encyclopedia of medieval thought, *Book of Contemplation* (1272), discussed for the first time in Romance language, theology, philosophy, moral and scientific subjects. Interpreting all reality as the manifestation of some aspect of the divinity, Llull taught theology, philosophy and the natural sciences as analogues of one another.

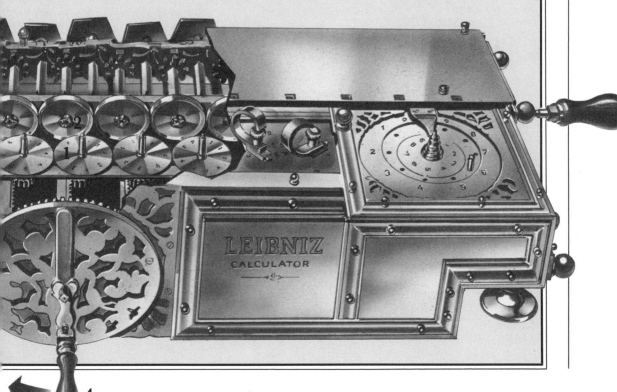

perfected the binary system of notation which is essential to the development of computers. Below: The Leibniz calculator was used for addition with numbered wheels for input (1) and a second set at right angles for output (2). For multiplication the same wheels were used, but with a different mechanism. The vital component was the stepped wheel (3), a cylindrical drum containing nine teeth of varying length. The mechanism was driven by a handle (4). Division was performed by operating the mechanism in reverse.

4

and inventing (and believing) the encouraging aphorism, "Everything is for the best in this best of all possible worlds." He also flirted, in a way that is most tantalizing to the historian who is obliged to wonder what would have happened if the flirtation had flowered into passion, with binary arithmetic.

Most human calculating is done, as everybody knows, according to the principles of decimal arithmetic. We begin counting from zero through to nine, and then start all over again prefacing the same ten digits with a 1, later with a 2,3,4 and so on. In other words we employ a maximum of ten symbols, including zero, and form any and every number out of permutations of these symbols. This may seem to be labouring the obvious, but it is necessary to do so because most people seem to think that this is the "natural" and perhaps even the *only* way to count. But what is special about ten? Why not an octal (based on eight) system for example? Using this one would have only eight symbols and would count 0,1,2,3,4,5,6,7, 10,11,12,13,14, 15,16,17, 20, etc. Actually the octal system has some nice features—it is very convenient, for example, that the key number halves and doubles neatly and indefinitely. This emphasizes the point that, though we currently count in tens, there's nothing inevitable or immutable about that. It is just one of a very large number of ways in which arithmetical systems can be built up. This fact is one of which all mathematicians are fully aware, and indeed were aware in the time of Leibniz, Pascal and others, but most of them were convinced of the virtues of the decimal system and could see no obvious reason for changing it. For a period Leibniz began to take a more than passing interest in a system of counting which, in fact, is one of the oldest known to man—the binary system. Here only two basic numbers are used, 0 and 1. There are no 3s, 4s, 5s, etc. Even so it is possible to express any number that can be expressed in the decimal—or any other system for that matter—using these two symbols. It is worth looking at this briefly because it helps one to grasp the basic principle of operation of all modern computers.

Binary arithmetic starts off quite straightforwardly, 0 being written 0 and 1 being written 1. But from there it moves rapidly away from conventional decimal notation. 2, for example, is 10, while 3 is 11 and 4 is 100. Remember that in the octal system there is no special symbol for 8, and after 7 the next number you write is 10. The same applies in binary, the only difference being that you get to the mathematical turning point, if it can be put in that way, after two numerals instead of eight. Now things get even stranger. There is no symbol for 5, so instead you write

101. 6 is 110; 7, 111 and 8 is 1000. 9 is 1001, 10, 1010, 11, 1011 and 12, 1100. For 13 we have 1101, 14, 1110 and 15, 1111. At 16 the number lengthens once again and we have 10000 while 17 is 10001 and so on. This may look a bit complicated and perhaps a bit mad, but the important thing to grasp is that with this system you can do mathematical notation using only *two* types of symbols, whereas, of course, in a decimal system you need ten. This may not be much of an advantage to human beings, and the long numbers which tend to build up using binary notation are difficult to comprehend at a glance. But for calculating machines, mechanical, electronic or otherwise, the picture is quite different. Nothing, just nothing, can be so convenient or appropriate as a binary system.

The reasons for this are obvious and striking if you consider the complex interior of even Pascal's simple calculator. Every single number up to ten had to be represented in his device by a tooth on a cog-wheel, and thus every cog-wheel had to have ten teeth. The same applied to other cog-wheels coping with the 10s, the 100s, the 1000s and so on, making for a mass of interconnecting gears, a vast increase in complexity, and a corresponding probability of mechanical error with every increase in the size of the device.

Now, as I have said, there was a brief period in his life when Leibniz turned his tremendous intellectual powers to bear on the utility and the potential of binary arithmetic, becoming fascinated with its elegance, economy and simplicity. At the same time his mind must have been at least partially preoccupied with the problems of the mechanical calculator and its already daunting complexity. What whim of fate prevented the two conceptual areas from blending together to produce what might have been one of the most dramatic advances in the history of scientific invention we shall never know. How would the future of calculating machines, the future of mathematics, the advance of computation and science have progressed if Leibniz had spotted that, instead of all those interlocking gears, one could have had a series of on-off binary levers or sprung switches, simple to design, cheap to build, easy to assemble and enormously reliable? Giant steam-driven computers in the nineteenth century perhaps? The beginning of the Industrial Revolution fifty years ahead of its time and in Germany instead of Britain? One can go on guessing endlessly, but there is little point in it. Leibniz's brain didn't oblige by integrating the two areas of possibility—and instead its owner for once got hold of the wrong end of the stick, and got hold of it quite firmly. The extreme elegance of the binary system lured him out of applied mathematics and into mystical and religious waters, and

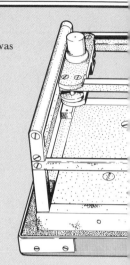

Left: **Charles, 3rd Earl Stanhope** (**1753–1816**), formerly Viscount Mahon, was an English radical politician and experimental scientist. He invented a cylindrical biconvex lens to eliminate spherical aberration, the first iron hand printing press and two calculating machines, both of which were intended primarily for performing multiplication and division by repeated addition and subtraction. The Earl sympathized with the French republicans and opposed the war with France following the Revolution, and strongly supported the democratization of Parliament.

instead of suggesting to him the possibility of dramatic advances in automatic calculation, it put into his mind the notion that the number one symbolized God, the all powerful and ever-present, and zero the empty universe. The end product was that he worked out a crude mathematical "proof" that God had created the world out of nothing. His colleagues in philosophy and the world of science weren't too impressed, but the Emperor of China was quite overcome when Leibniz tried it out on him. Thus binary arithmetic made its first real mark on the world through the conversion of the Chinese Emperor.

There was little advance in the development of automatic calculating machines for about a century. This was not because there was anything faulty about the Pascal/Leibniz type of design, but because the component wheels and gears needed to be constructed to a tolerance which taxed the embryonic skills of the metal-workers of the time.

In the meanwhile interest began to grow in the interesting area of symbolic logic. Logic, which is concerned with the rules of argument, or what one can and cannot reasonably infer from a particular set of circumstances, lends itself to formalization, and at about this time a number of people were beginning to work seriously on this formalizing task. The principles of logic—much simpler than those governing most mathematical procedures, incidentally—were also sufficiently clear-cut to tempt various minds to the problem of devising a machine to employ them automatically. One such device, and almost certainly the first, was demonstrated in the late 1770s by the statesman/scientist the Earl of Stanhope. Stanhope had already come up with an automatic calculator somewhat easier to operate than Pascal's but packed out, as usual, with gears and wheels. His "Logic Demonstrator" had no real moving parts and

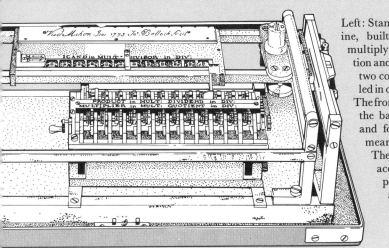

consisted of a block of wood with a glass window in the centre of it. Behind the wood were two slides, one coloured grey, which represented the first premise of whatever argument was being logically analysed, and the other red, to represent the second premise. To arrive at a logical conclusion, believe it or not, one moved the slides to various positions behind the window and read off their relative position against two numbered scales. Perhaps it is a bit much to call this a machine as all the judging or computation is done by the operator, but the gadget was interesting inasmuch as it suggested that sooner or later, provided that one could get a proper "calculus of logic", one ought to be able to build logical analysers into machines which would allow them to make decisions of a logical nature.

The really big breakthrough in this area came later from the mathematician George Boole, who was the first to demonstrate clearly that logic was a branch of mathematics and not of philosophy as it had been previously assumed. He backed this up with a magnificent extension of algebraic method (Boolean algebra), which was the first to use algebraic symbols to denote *operations* (i.e., "do this", not "and", "if", "or", etc.) as distinguished from *quantity* (i.e. sums and numbers). Boole's name is a household word among computer scientists and mathematicians and his influence on the development of computers and their rules of operation was unique, and yet he is virtually unknown outside these fields. It would be a moral error to write anything about the past, present and future of computers without sending a thought spinning off in his direction.

And so the eighteenth century, full of economic and political upheaval, came to a close. In its last decade, however, Charles Babbage, one of the world's most remarkable inventors, was born.

Below: **George Boole (1815–64)**, English logician and mathematician, showed in his

Mathematical Analysis of Logic (1847) and *Investigation of the Laws of Thought* (1854) the relationship of mathematics and logic; his algebra of logic (Boolean algebra) enabled a variety of logical problems to be dealt with as algebraic operations. Son of a tradesman, Boole started a school before being appointed Professor of Mathematics at Cork in 1849, despite having no degree. An outstanding pioneer of modern symbolic logic, he was awarded the Royal Medal by the Royal Society in 1844 and elected a Fellow in 1857.

The Father of Computing

So far, I have been using words like calculator, mechanical adder, computer and so on to mean much the same thing, and no doubt this will have bothered the purists. But I have done it deliberately because I wanted, first and foremost, to emphasize the most important single fact about calculators, computers or whatever other name you like to give them: they are really only devices which represent numbers or quantities as physical states, and which juggle these numbers or quantities around by changing these physical states. A physical state, just to ram the message home, can be a gear-wheel in a particular position, a lever either up or down, a switch on or off, the presence or absence of an electrical charge in a vacuum tube, a current pulsating in a wire, a magnetic substance in a magnetized or unmagnetized condition, and so on and so forth. In the early days of automatic calculators these "states" more or less *had* to be of the gear-wheel variety because that was the only way in which man could construct devices consisting of interlocking units capable of interacting with each other and changing their states as required. Later, electronic components were introduced into calculators with enormous changes in efficiency, and we shall get on to these in a later chapter.

Let us look once again at the crudest kind of calculator, the abacus. It has moving parts in the form of a set of beads which can be moved around on a frame to represent different numbers. And that's about all. The abacus can't move on its own and it doesn't do any kind of calculation in itself. All the effort has to come from the user, who takes the first part of the sum, sets it by moving the beads into position, and then takes the second part of the sum and moves the beads accordingly into their new position. If the sum is a large one he will almost certainly have to move extra beads in order to cope with the carrying function. When he's finished, he looks at where the beads are and, knowing the "code" of the abacus, interprets its "answer". Now let us return to Pascal's little brainchild. Here you set up the sum by dialling in the various numbers to be computed, and the human doesn't have to do any special coding. The action of dialling in the numbers causes the gears to move around marvellously inside the box, and, lo! at a set of small windows various numbers appear. You read these and there is your answer. It is clear that the calculation, simple though it may be, has actually been performed by the machine through the interaction of the various parts of its innards, and what is more their interaction has been specially decoded to give an answer in terms any user can understand. The Pascaline, therefore, and its early successors, including Leibniz's model, is a machine with a number of features. Firstly it has an input device—the dials for entry of the numbers. Secondly it has a set of calculating mechanisms—the gears and their interconnecting parts. Thirdly it has an output device—the dials on which one reads the final sum. In this way it is actually rather close to a modern computer, in concept if not in power and complexity. On the other hand it is missing three features or component units which must be present in any machine which can properly be called a computer. The first of these is that it has no memory. The second is that it has no decision-making unit (called the central processor in modern computer usage). The third is that it lacks functional flexibility—it is not programmable. The exact meaning and significance of these terms will gradually become clear as we proceed, and as we take up the tale of Charles Babbage.

Babbage was an inventor and a mathematician of eminence, born in England in 1792. He was, like many of the scholars of the time, a man of considerable wealth, having inherited over £100,000 on his father's death, but just about every penny of it vanished into the mad, gallant enterprise which became his life's work. Like many mathematicians Babbage had a tidy—perhaps obsessively tidy—mind. Inaccuracies and imprecision bothered him greatly, and he spent a good deal of time writing petulant notes to scientific societies drawing attention to trifling errors which had crept into their published data and computation tables. The growing complexity of life, even in the days preceding the Industrial Revolution, was already beginning to make itself felt and more and more people made their living solely on the basis of performing routine calculations, checking other people's lists and tables, and compiling numerical data of all kinds. Among the most arduous and error-prone tasks of this kind was the compilation of log tables, and Babbage was forever spotting trivial errors in them which, because of the peculiar nature of logarithms, would compound to massive errors in the final sums produced. According to his own account—the somehow moving little passage that is quoted at the beginning of this book—it was pondering the time-wasting and desperately routine nature of log calculations which led him to conceive that a machine ought to be able to do it far more easily and far more accurately. Before long the basic scheme for such a machine began to assemble itself in his mind, and in 1821 he was sufficiently confident of what he was doing to announce to the Royal Astronomical Society that he would build a pilot model and demonstrate it to them. The machine would work, he indicated, "on the method of differences", and he gave convincing details as to how it would actually go about its business. We don't need to explain exactly how it worked, except to say that it could solve polynomial equations by calculating successive differences between sets of numbers. He showed the working model to the assembled Society in 1822 and the presentation was so well received that his paper "Observations on the Application of Machinery to the Computation of Mathematical Tables" was awarded the Society's gold medal—its first. Little did those elegantly whiskered astronomers, now long dead, realize just how significant was the event they were commemorating.

Even the sketchiest glance at Babbage's plans reveals that it was a very ambitious scheme indeed. The basic principles of calculation—cogs and wheels again—were really no different from anything that had been built before, and there are some close similarities between features of the Difference Engine and the calculator built by the Earl of Stanhope a few decades earlier. But it was going to be *very* much bigger and *very* much more complicated, and with his limitless optimism Babbage had determined that it should not only calculate tables but also print them out on paper at the end. In 1823 the British Government awarded the first of a very long string of grants to support the development of computers and handed him a cheque for £1500. A workshop was built on Babbage's estate, skilled workmen hired and construction got under way.

The main task, apart from the design specification and drawings, was the turning up on special lathes, and to the highest possible tolerances, of the hundreds of rods, wheels, ratchets and gears which would constitute the Difference Engine's working parts. And it was here that Babbage began to hit his first big snags. The little unit which he had built for the Astronomical Society was merely a demonstration piece with a limited number of components and crude computational power. Minor irregularities in its components might lead to a certain amount of slack in the system, but these would be too insignificant to cause any jamming or inhibit its overall function. But in the Difference Engine proper it was another matter. Any series of minor imperfections tended to compound, leading to great internal shakings and seizures. Babbage tightened up the manufacturing specification, and urged his workers to greater and greater care. There was an improvement, but not enough to match the overall complexity of the system. Undaunted by his first setbacks, perhaps stubbornly so, Babbage lashed his mechanics in a vain attempt to make them perform better than the tools and materials of the time would allow, and applied to the Government for more and more money. They obliged up to a total of £17,000 and then decided that enough was enough. Babbage could no longer pay his long-suffering craftsmen and the project went into suspended animation in 1833.

Now if Babbage had been a sensible man—which he wasn't—this is the moment when he would have sat back and surveyed the tons of brass and pewter cog-wheels, sprockets and other knick-knacks and faced up to the fact that he was a hundred years ahead of his time—which he was. But instead of doing what commonsense and all his colleagues, friends and relations urged him to do, his restless mind began to consider an even more ambitious scheme: the construction of something he called an Analytical Engine. And at that moment the concept of the computer was born.

Although the Difference Engine was an order of magnitude more advanced than anything that had been attempted in the way of automatic calculation in the past, it was still basically a calculator rather than a computer. It was capable of doing just one job—solving polynomial equations. And this it achieved by going through a fixed set of movements, the turning of one set of wheels inducing the turning of another set, one lever raising another and so on, all in a more or less predictable sequence. The system in other words was similar to what would now be called a special-purpose computer. It had one job it could do, and that was all it lived for.

Pondering this, Babbage saw it was far from being the whole story. A machine which could perform genuine calculations of one kind could, in all probability, perform *any* kind of calculation—a hunch which was to be demonstrated mathematically over a century later by another British genius, Alan Turing. A radical and exciting concept now emerged. Why not make a single machine which didn't have a fixed purpose, but which could tackle any or all of these tasks as and when the owner wanted it to? It might be a lot more complicated than the Difference Engine, and a lot more expensive to build (Babbage's optimistic temperament allowed him to skim over boring financial matters with ease), but it would be a whole lot more useful. The "obvious" thought must have been to see the new machine as a composite of lots of other machines, part "a" coming into being for task "a", and part "b" for task "b", but all of them using, say, a common input mechanism and a common link to the printer or other output device. But once again Babbage rejected the obvious and in doing so came to his magnificent insight. The machine's design should be such that its internal parts could be employed in a great variety of different ways, so that when a particular task was being tackled a unique sequence of internal activity would be set up, with each different task being tied to unique internal "patterns of action". All that was needed was a clever idea for telling the machine which of the infinite variety of "patterns of action" were to be employed at any one time. This wonderous device was the Analytical Engine, and it's worth interjecting that what he was talking about was a programmable computer. A program, of course, is nothing more than a series of instructions to a machine telling it what to do with itself—what patterns of action or calculation its interlocking components must generate in order to solve a particular problem.

This is not a book about how computers work and I will not attempt to explain the frenetic complexities of the interior of the Analytical Engine. Descriptions of it abound, one of the best being by an engineer in the Italian army, L. F. Menabrea, which was later translated into English by the Countess of Lovelace. Best of all, for those who really want to get a feeling for the scope and ambition of the project, there exists a model of part of it in the Science Museum in London, where it has pride of place among a quite magnificent collection of early computers and calculating machines. On the other hand it is worth looking briefly into the guts of the Analytical Engine if only to spot that it consisted of a number of distinct and partly autonomous functioning units, which are very close to the functioning units of all modern computers.

In the first place, it had a set of input devices—methods of feeding numbers or instructions into its interior. Secondly, it had an arithmetical unit, or processor, which was the part of the machine that actually calculated the numbers. Babbage called this the mill. Thirdly, there was a control unit which ensured that the computer performed one task rather than another and completed all the calculations in the correct sequence. Fourthly, it had a store or memory, where numbers could be held to wait their turn to be processed. Finally, there was the output mechanism itself. And there, rather oversimplified, are the five essential components of any computer, ancient or modern. For his calculation and memory devices Babbage had to rely on the good old standby of column after column of ten-toothed wheels, hooked up to the mill by a quite incredible collection of rods and linkages.

The prototype Difference Engine was hand-powered. One moved a lever to set the innards churning and a bell rang when that particular stage of the calculation had been achieved. One then fed in whatever else one had to, moved

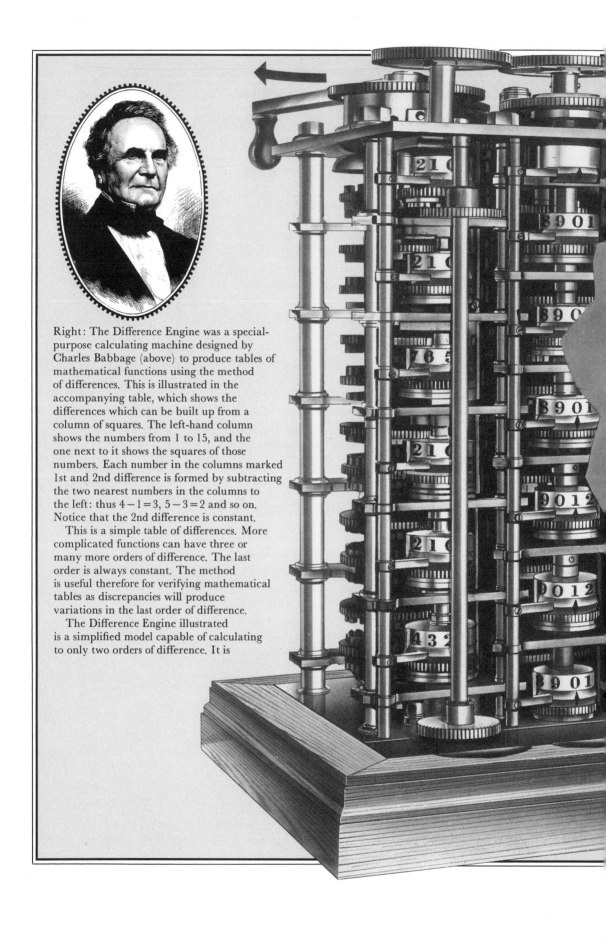

Right: The Difference Engine was a special-purpose calculating machine designed by Charles Babbage (above) to produce tables of mathematical functions using the method of differences. This is illustrated in the accompanying table, which shows the differences which can be built up from a column of squares. The left-hand column shows the numbers from 1 to 15, and the one next to it shows the squares of those numbers. Each number in the columns marked 1st and 2nd difference is formed by subtracting the two nearest numbers in the columns to the left: thus $4 - 1 = 3$, $5 - 3 = 2$ and so on. Notice that the 2nd difference is constant.

This is a simple table of differences. More complicated functions can have three or many more orders of difference. The last order is always constant. The method is useful therefore for verifying mathematical tables as discrepancies will produce variations in the last order of difference.

The Difference Engine illustrated is a simplified model capable of calculating to only two orders of difference. It is

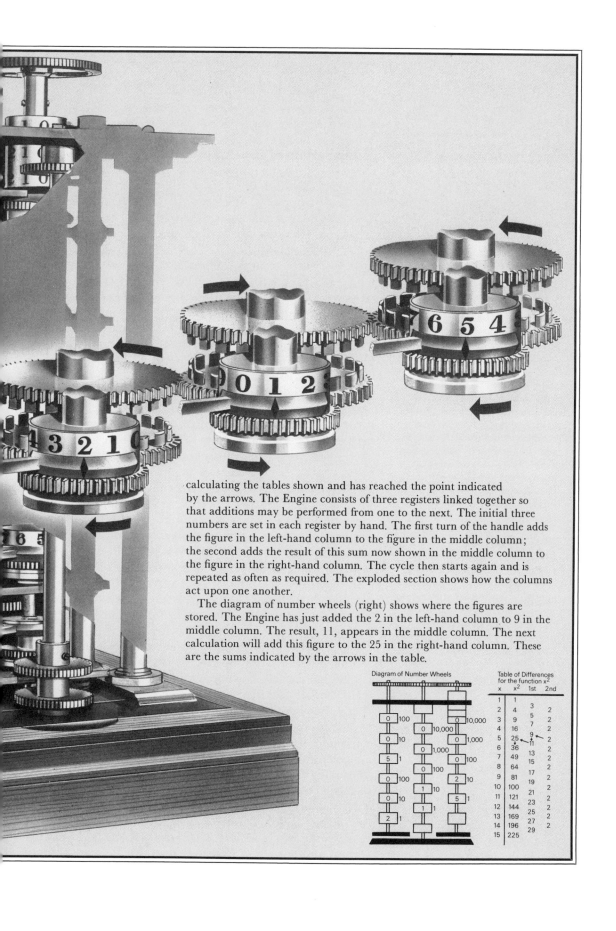

calculating the tables shown and has reached the point indicated
by the arrows. The Engine consists of three registers linked together so
that additions may be performed from one to the next. The initial three
numbers are set in each register by hand. The first turn of the handle adds
the figure in the left-hand column to the figure in the middle column;
the second adds the result of this sum now shown in the middle column to
the figure in the right-hand column. The cycle then starts again and is
repeated as often as required. The exploded section shows how the columns
act upon one another.

The diagram of number wheels (right) shows where the figures are
stored. The Engine has just added the 2 in the left-hand column to 9 in the
middle column. The result, 11, appears in the middle column. The next
calculation will add this figure to the 25 in the right-hand column. These
are the sums indicated by the arrows in the table.

Diagram of Number Wheels

Table of Differences
for the function x^2

x	x^2	1st	2nd
1	1		
2	4	3	2
3	9	5	2
4	16	7	2
5	25	9	2
6	36	11	2
7	49	13	2
8	64	15	2
9	81	17	2
10	100	19	2
11	121	21	2
12	144	23	2
13	169	25	2
14	196	27	2
15	225	29	

Charles Babbage (1792–1871), English mathematician and inventor, has been heralded the Father of Computing after his invention of the Analytical Engine. As the son of a wealthy Devon banker, Babbage was able to devote himself to research. The idea of calculating mathematical tables mechanically came to him in around 1812, and thereafter he devoted nearly 40 years and a large part of his own fortune together with Government grants to this project, ultimately in vain. His first conception was the Difference Engine, but before this was completed Babbage conceived the much more ambitious Analytical Engine, which was truly programmable and is recognizable as a computer. It would have been steam-driven and programmed by means of machined cards, but was never completed. Had Babbage the benefit of electricity the development of the computer might have been a very different story. He was instrumental in the formation of the Royal Astronomical and Statistical Societies; elected a Fellow of the Royal Society in 1816; and was Lucasian professor of mathematics at Cambridge University from 1828 to 1839. He published papers on mathematics, statistics, physics and geology, compiled the first actuarial tables, was instrumental in the development of the penny post and invented the speedometer and the locomotive cowcatcher—a protective device fitted to locomotives to guard against cows and bullocks on the line. Babbage also invented an ophthalmoscope, a medical instrument used for the examination of eyes, but failed to make it work.

the lever again until the bell rang, and so on. Babbage had no illusions about the physical awkwardness of this and had planned to use steam power for his later version, the Analytical Engine. Now, if there's something partly pathetic and partly laughable about the notion of coupling the noisy, surging power of a steam engine to the numinous matter of calculating numbers, then this merely serves as another example of the fact that Babbage was really dreaming—dreaming magnificently it is true, but still dreaming—decades ahead of his time.

For the input and to program instructions to the control unit, he leant on an invention of the Frenchman Joseph Jacquard. Jacquard had realized that when weavers of cloth were controlling their looms, they were performing a delicate, skilled, but nevertheless essentially repetitive task, and that it ought to be possible to automate the control process. For this he devised a stiff card with a series of holes punched in it in a particular pattern. In the course of weaving, a series of rods carry the threads into the loom, and the role of the punched card was to block some of these rods and let those which slipped through the holes go on to complete the weave. At each throw of the shuttle a single card with a particular pattern of holes appeared in the path of the rods, thus controlling the pattern of the weave. It could also be described as a program controlling the loom, and Babbage realized that it could equally well be employed to control the sequence of calculations within his Engine. Jacquard's invention, by the way, received much the same response as had the spinning jenny in England at an earlier date. The weavers complained that it would put them out of work and beat up Jacquard's apparatus whenever they could lay their hands on it; once in a while they even beat up Jacquard. It may not have been an auspicious beginning to programming, but punched cards have controlled big automatic calculators and computers ever since and they are only now beginning to slide out of fashion.

The parallel with weaving was also spotted by Ada, Countess of Lovelace, whom we met briefly earlier on as the translator of Menabrea's commentary. "The Analytical Engine weaves algebraical patterns just as the Jacquard loom weaves flowers and leaves," she remarked about Babbage's proposed machine. This intriguing woman was an exceptional mathematician and was by all accounts an unusually beautiful one into the bargain. A contemporary sketch shows her to have something of the looks of Elizabeth Taylor and more than a trace of the handsome features of her father, Lord Byron. When she met Babbage, and realized the significance of what he was trying to do and the gallant and dogged optimism with which he was trying to

Left: The Analytical Engine designed by Charles Babbage is recognized as the world's first general-purpose computer, even though it never got beyond the design stage. The Engine was to have consisted of a calculating unit (the mill), a memory (the store), an input device and a control section (both based on Jacquard punched cards) and a printer. The machine shown here is a small part of the Engine constructed just before Babbage died by his son Henry; it consists of a small part of the mill and the printer.

do it, she fell in love with him more or less on the spot. She exerted an encouraging and stabilizing influence on him at a time when he had every right to be sitting about gloomily complaining about how badly the world was treating him. She set out to study his designs for the Analytical Engine in depth, filling in any blank spots by pulling them out of his head in conversation. She had money and time on her side, being both wealthy and in her twenties, but even so it was a few years before she got it all together. When she did, she published everything in a long series of "Notes" entitled "Observations on Mr Babbage's Analytical Engine". They make excellent reading if you want to study his enterprise in detail, and Babbage himself said she "seems to understand it better than I do, and is far, far better at explaining it". She also showed that she was aware of some of the philosophical problems which the construction of such a machine posed, and which have not really been resolved today. For example, on the question of whether the machine could be considered to be creative or not she wrote:

The Analytical Engine has no pretensions whatever to originate anything. It can do whatever we know how to order it to perform. It can follow analysis; but it has no power of anticipating any analytical relations or truths. Its province is to assist us in making available what we are already acquainted with.

42

Right: **Joseph-Marie Jacquard (1752–1834)**, French silk-weaver, invented the Jacquard loom in 1801, which was significant not only because it started the transformation of the textile industry to its modern scale but because the loom used punched cards to control the weaving of patterns in the cloth —the forerunners of the cards used in modern data storage systems. The success of the loom, to this day the basis of modern automatic looms, inspired both Babbage (1792–1871) and Hollerith (1860–1929) and, through them, the data processing and computer industries. The completion of the loom was delayed by the French Revolution (in which Jacquard fought on the side of the revolutionaries), but he was finally rewarded with a state pension and a royalty on each machine, and subsequently the Légion d'Honneur. Threatened as a work force, the weavers were less favourably impressed and destroyed several of the machines—indeed on one occasion Jacquard was lucky to escape with his life.

It is a very perceptive comment and seems to be the first ever statement of the argument which today crops up unfailingly whenever the intellectual potential of computers is discussed—a computer can only do what you program it to. This is an attractive, but only superficially powerful argument, but all credit to Lady Lovelace for making it first.

The real significance of her Notes was probably in the effect they had on Babbage. Up to this point, apart from his triumph with the Astronomical Society, he was akin to the one-eyed man in the country of the Blind. He knew that he was working on something of immense, perhaps eternal, importance, but had rarely bumped up against anyone who approved of what he was doing, let alone understood it. What was particularly gratifying to him was that Lady Lovelace had taken the trouble to study his theoretical approach with the eye of a mathematician and had found no flaws in it. He knew the Analytical Engine would work (in principle) and now she knew it too. All that remained was to get the wretched thing built—which was turning out to be horribly difficult.

In the meantime there had been a change of government in England and the Treasury had given up financing what they now believed was a hopeless project—remember they were still waiting for the Difference Engine to be completed. In 1842 Babbage managed to get an interview with the Prime Minister, Sir Robert Peel, to ask for funds, but Peel was not sympathetic and had no real understanding of what he was trying to achieve. Babbage stormed out of his office in a huff. The Prime Minister, adopting a strategy which had often worked in the past to placate disgruntled madmen who felt the Government owed them something, offered Babbage a knighthood. He turned this down quite impolitely, and went back to wrestle with the problems of the Analytical Engine and seek what emotional and intellectual support he could get in the company of Lady Lovelace. But by now the tide of his life, luck and spirit was beginning to ebb. Money became tighter, friends less helpful and communicative, critics more scathing and scientific colleagues less tolerant and understanding. Only Ada stood by him, continuously compiling notes and lobbying for support with her friends of influence. Not all her assistance was beneficial, however. At one stage she seems to have got bitten with that peculiarly insidious bug—mathematicians are as prey to it as bus drivers—and came to believe that she had worked out a "system" which would allow her to place unfailingly winning bets on horse-races. This belief, held with her usual passion and conviction, cost her an awful lot of money before she was cured of it and Babbage lost some of his own shrinking reserves in the same fever.

Time went by. The Difference Engine remained an incomplete assembly of gears and cams, the Analytical Engine a series of paper sketches, mental concepts and Lady Lovelace's Notes. The tide ebbed faster. At the age of thirty-six Ada died and Babbage pressed on alone, achieving little. Governments came and went, none any more sympathetic to his ideas. Disraeli even wrote scathingly that the only possible use he could see for the Difference Engine was to calculate the vast sums of money that had been squandered on it. Babbage counter-attacked, criticizing the Government for its lack of conception of science and education and turning on the Royal Society, which he believed had betrayed him. He was not the only true genius whose golden contribution to society has been dismissed as dross, but knowing that one is not alone in being misunderstood by blockheads is not really all that much comfort.

The problem, of course, was that he was ahead of the

Below: **Augusta Ada, Countess of Lovelace (1815–52)**, was the only child of Lord Byron (1788–1824) and Anne Isabella Milbanke, who left Byron in 1816. Byron saw himself as a gloomy romantic figure and was given to dramatization. He wrote to his half-sister Augusta on 8 October 1823: "I hope that the Gods have made her [Ada] any thing save *poetical*—it is enough to have one such fool in a family." Ada, however, was apparently a happy child despite her nervous disposition and constant poor health. It is clear from Lady

Lovelace's sophisticated and perceptive work on Babbage's ideas, *Observations on Mr Babbage's Analytical Engine*, that Byron's fears were indeed unfounded. Such mathematical talent may well have been inherited from her mother, who was described by her husband as the "Princess of Parallelograms". Although Ada's scientific and mathematical talents were utilized in her association with Babbage, they were ultimately abused by their application to gambling on horses which led to blackmail and caused Ada to pawn some of the family jewels.

Below: The Scheutz Difference Engine No. 2 was built in Bermondsey by Messrs Bryan Donkin from the drawings of Edvard Scheutz, following a commission from the General Register Office, which used the machine to compute life expectancy tables. It is much more powerful than the Babbage machine pictured on pages 38–9, and is very different in design. The calculating part consists of five rows of numbered rings, with 15 rings in each row. The upper row registers the result of the calculation, and the remaining rows register the first, second, third and fourth order of difference descending from the top. As with Babbage's machine, the initial figures are set by hand, then the handle is turned to start the cycle of calculation, which proceeds as long as desired. The Scheutz Engine printed out its results to the first eight of the 15 figures onto a strip of sheet lead or papier mâché, from which stereotype plates were prepared for use in an ordinary printing press.

technology of his time—in the Analytical Engine by many decades, perhaps even a century, and in the Difference Engine also, though to a lesser extent. Any independent mathematician or engineer reading the available accounts of the two devices could see that both were, in principle, sound and could form the basis of machines that might be constructed. But whereas the Analytical Engine would be the more adventurous and, once built, far more powerful, its sheer complexity and the vast number of its interlocking parts tended to set the mind spinning. The Difference Engine, on the other hand, might easily be built—indeed, the working model which had impressed the Astronomical Society as far back as 1822 was there to prove it.

Independent mathematicians and engineers *did* read Babbage's publications and Lady Lovelace's Notes, and with great interest. One of these was a Swedish engineer by the name of Georg Scheutz, who in 1834 came across the account of the Difference Engine published in the *Edinburgh Review*. Now Swedes, as anyone who owns a Volvo knows, like making neat, chunky bits of machinery which work well, and Scheutz set out to build his own version of the Difference Engine. So successful was he that he was able to produce a reliable working design suitable for manufacturing and sale and exhibited the first "production model" in 1855. Among the crowds who gathered round this curious device—you can see it now with its funny systems of wheels, weights, and trolleys for "carrying" numbers in the Science Museum in London—was Babbage himself, now aged sixty-three and a very disheartened individual. When asked to comment on the Scheutz machine, he was gallantly congratulatory, but it is not easy nor comfortable to speculate on the thoughts that must have passed through his mind as he saw those Swedish wheels turning, the levers moving and the results of the calculations being printed out

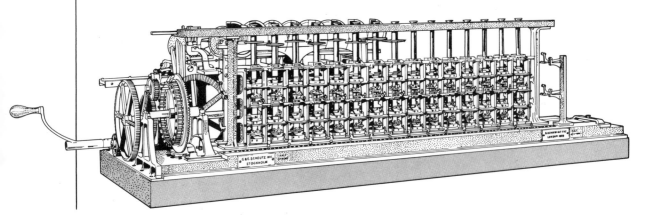

laboriously, but accurately, at the end. The final blow came when the British Government actually bought one to assist in the calculation of life expectancy tables for the Registrar-General's office, while at about the same time that part of Babbage's Difference Engine which had actually been put together was exhibited at the Great Industrial Exhibition in London, tucked away in an ignominious position.

In 1871 Babbage died and it is both safe and sad to say that he died a disappointed man, but he had grasped a concept so exciting and so revolutionary that it would some day change the world; and while, deep down, he must have known that his vision was premature, he also knew that it was a great and true vision. He had seen, though it must have been unimaginably galling for him to do so, the off-spring of his Difference Engine in the form of Scheutz's Calculating Machine in production and actually going to work doing something useful. For a man of his insight and lucidity, this would simply have served to confirm his own lifelong belief that machines would eventually eliminate the need for mind-clogging routine calculation, and ultimately enrich the intellectual life of man. His contemporaries seem to have dismissed him as a misguided, irascible and un-reasonable genius, but a genius beyond all doubt. So certain of his brilliance was everyone that his brain was removed after his death. In 1907 a detailed examination was made of it to see if it had any physical characteristics which marked it off clearly from other men. One of the leading surgeons of the time, Sir Victor Horsley, undertook the examination and, after prodding around among the millions of silent neurones, announced that it seemed to him to be no different from any other brain he had seen. No one wanted to throw it away, however, and it is still preserved, in two jars of pickle, one for each hemisphere, in the Hunterian Museum at the Royal College of Surgeons, where you will be shown it if you ask nicely.

But if you think that by looking at it you will in some way be close to Charles Babbage, think again. The dead brain is just a bunch of lifeless neural tissue, barely worth the jars it is preserved in and nothing to do with Babbage at all. If you really want to contact his ghost, then stand in the centre of a giant computer complex where the data lights flicker as the machine hunts through its megabytes of memory, or hold in the palm of your hand a chip containing a hundred thousand logic gates. Best of all, invest in one of the build-your-own-computer kits that are now becoming a hobbyist rage, and assemble it all—input terminal, memory, central processor, etc.—on your kitchen table. If you do this and you have the right kind of way of looking at things, you may find Babbage at your elbow.

Below: **Georg Scheutz** (1785–1873), Swedish engineer, built a simplified version of Babbage's Difference Engine with his son Edvard (1821–81). It was exhibited at the Paris Exhibition of 1855, winning a gold medal. A copy commissioned by the

British government was completed in 1859 and used in the Registrar-General's Office. Its main task, the calculation of actuarial tables used for predicting life expectancy, was completed in 1864.

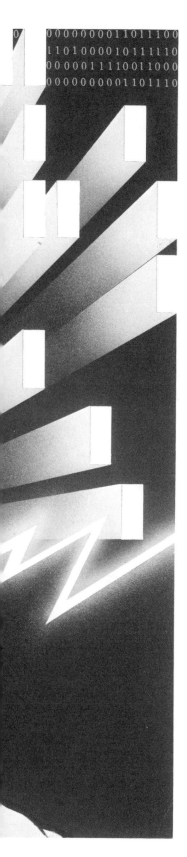

Computers in Harness

By 1871, at the time Charles Babbage died, the focus of industrial growth and commercial success was showing the first signs of shifting from Europe to the United States. This was a fact which, had it been known, would have been neither comprehensible nor palatable to the European powers—notably Great Britain, which was then seemingly at the height of its imperial strength. Its economy was growing by leaps and bounds, its people's affluence was soaring and its grasp of world industry unchallenged. A hundred years of leadership of the Industrial Revolution had made its mark.

But the huge potential of the North American continent was also beginning to reveal itself. The destructive Civil War had been resolved, mines and factories were booming and the West had been opened up to provide food and mineral wealth on a scale that no other country could begin to match. In addition, an expanding communications network with a common language was beginning to unite Americans into one enormously powerful democracy, in striking contrast to the continent of Europe with its strutting, warring, endlessly competing nations whose multiplicity of tongues and bureaucratic barriers hampered travel and commerce. America, in particular the United States, was reaping the reward of these economic and political imbalances by creaming off through immigration a steady tide of the most ambitious, bold and imaginative of Europe's citizens, and its population swelled accordingly.

These new hordes posed formidable problems to those sections of the US administration that were concerned with recording and documentation. Congress had stipulated that a census and complete update was to be taken every ten years, and this placed a nightmare burden on those who had to do the counting, checking and recording. The eleventh census was held in 1880 and the task of making sense of it began. Two, three and four years passed without any concrete conclusions and when, in 1887, data was still being processed the Census Office realized (a) that the results, when completed, would be hopelessly out of date; (b) that they might not all be in by the time of the next census; and (c) that the problems with the next census would be significantly greater than those of the present one.

Part of the problem was the burgeoning population, amplified by the fact that the immigrants moved around pretty much at will in the early stages, trying out city after

Above: Hollerith's punched card equipment cut the time taken to process the 1890 census to a third of that taken over the 1880 figures.

city until they had found something to suit. A multiplicity of details also had to be gathered about education, family size, ethnic origins, literacy and occupation, but worst of all was the hopelessly inefficient way in which this information was being handled. Firstly the data had to be captured —an inescapable chore—and after that it had to be broken down or coded in some way—an enormous task, riddled with opportunities for error. Then everything had to be counted, yielding great sets of numbers which in turn had to be converted back into meaningful statistics. No matter which way the Census Bureau looked at it, things couldn't go on like this, and they were forced to consider a radically different approach. This, incidentally, probably represented the moment when a group of human beings first realized that their world was getting so complex that it was now beyond the power of the human brain, unaided, to analyse.

The solution was to hold a competition to find an improved form of recording and counting. There were a large number of entries, some pretty mad as is usual in this kind of public free-for-all, but a few really ingenious. In the end a shortlist of three was drawn up featuring Mr William C. Hunt and his coloured cards, Mr Charles F. Pidgin and his colour-coded tokens, and Mr Herman Hollerith and his amazing tabulating machine. Tradition favoured the first two and there were numerous voices raised against the idea of such data being entrusted to a machine. The contest was settled by a practical test in the city of St Louis, Missouri: the Hollerith method was over 50% better than its nearest rival in the overall task, and sensationally better when it came to the actual tabulation. Hunt's cards had taken 55 hours, Pidgin's tokens 44 hours and Hollerith's machine only $5\frac{1}{2}$ hours. All scepticism was routed and the Hollerith system was selected for the 1890 census.

Although we are now talking about a time only forty years after Babbage had been wrestling so miserably and to so little avail with the problem of building his Difference Engine, it will be plain from the above that there had been a sudden advance in the field of automatic computation. A number of factors had indeed changed. Firstly, machining and manufacturing skill, accelerating on the heels of the Industrial Revolution, had improved to the point where making boxes full of gears, cogs and cams which interfaced contentedly with each other had become feasible. Secondly, the business climate was more open towards the notion of machine computation, again spurred by the realization that modern, industrialized society would be unable to survive on pencil-and-paper computation alone. Thirdly, and in many ways this is the most important feature, a new form of motive power—electricity—had turned up, and this was almost ideally suited to the driving of large mechanical calculators.

In fact, a monster machine, otherwise similar to the Difference Engine, which could be powered by electricity had been made by an American engineer named George Barnard Grant and exhibited at the Centennial Exposition in Philadelphia in 1876. It was the size of a grand piano and required a lot of power to make it go, plus more or less constant supervision and intervention at the various stages of the calculation. People were very impressed by the fact that it worked, but they were also pretty impressed with the fact that it obviously had no place in any office or business environment, and that a stand in the Centennial Exposition was about as close to the real world as it would ever get. Grant himself wasn't dismayed, for he had seen the construction of his machine as a challenge to his engineering and mechanical skills—he was an expert, perhaps *the* expert, on the design and construction of tiny gears and cogs. The fact that his "Difference Engine" worked and Babbage's did not, and could not, reflects the advances in the various aspects of metal casting and working which had taken place in the critical decades of the middle of the nineteenth century.

But having proved to himself what could be done, Grant now set out to design and build smaller, more practical machines and he was immediately successful. One model known as the "Rack and Pinion Calculator" was quite small and moderately inexpensive, and he built and sold 125 of them. Even so, this machine suffered from two drawbacks which had been endemic in calculators since the beginning: the entry of the numbers to be calculated was a fiddly, time-consuming business, and the act of multiplication—which was probably the facet of computing that most begged for automation—was performed laboriously and required two or more intervening operations by the user. Both these handicaps were more or less eliminated in the 1880s, and at that point calculators really began to take off.

In the first place, a Spaniard by the name of Ramon Verea invented a system of "direct multiplication", which meant that only one manual operation was needed for each number in

Below: This calculator, patented by Frank Baldwin in 1875, embodied a vital technological breakthrough; the stepped wheel was replaced by a wheel that had nine spring-loaded pins on its edge. This eliminated the need for reversing gears to switch from addition or multiplication to subtraction or division.

Calculation was performed by entering the starting number via the levers in the slotted cylinder and turning the handle, which registered the number in the results window at the front. Addition required the levers to be reset to show the second number, and the handle turned clockwise once. Multiplication was performed by turning the handle as many times as required to complete the sum; the multiplier then showed in the window in the front casing. Subtraction and division worked in the same way, with the handle turned anti-clockwise.

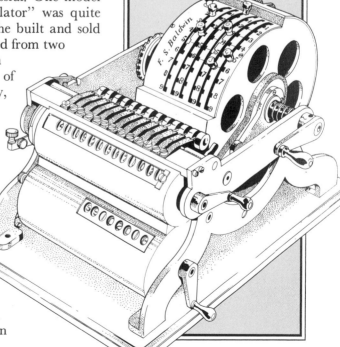

George Barnard Grant
(**1849–1917**), American inventor
and mechanical engineer,
became interested in calculating
machines while a student at
Harvard. Before he had
graduated he had taken out his
first patents, and had published
a paper describing his own
design for a Difference Engine,
which was exhibited in
Philadelphia in 1876. He also
worked on arithmetic calculators,
and produced two models, the
Barrel or Centennial, and the
Rack and Pinion, of which 125
were sold. His work with
calculating machines led him
into a close examination of
engineering methods, and he
subsequently became one of the
founders of the American gear-
cutting industry.

Below: The Rack and Pinion
was significant because it was a
reliable design which did much
to gain public confidence in the
principle of calculating
machines. Operation was
simple—figures were entered on
the wheels on the drum, the
handle was turned and the
results appeared on the wheels at
the front.

the multiplier, and this massively simplified matters. Verea
never really capitalized on his invention, and a Swiss
engineer named Otto Steiger was the first to put together a
direct multiplier. It was extremely reliable and, manufactured under the name of the "Millionaire", was sold
widely to Government agencies in the USA. It had a long
production life: the first was marketed in 1894 and the
4655th and last in the year 1935.

But even the Millionaire was fiddly to operate as the
numbers had to be set up on a kind of sliding scale. A vast
improvement came when an American, Dorr E. Felt,
produced a key-addressed device—the numbers were
punched in on a set of keys rather like those of a typewriter
—which he named the "Comptometer". This proved so
easy to use and so popular with clerks that vast numbers of
them were sold to Government agencies and big business
organizations, and the Comptometer might have swept the
board had it not been for a rival system invented by William
Burroughs. Felt had realized that for his machine to fulfil
its potential properly it ought not only to calculate but
also to print out its results on paper, and to achieve this he
developed a workable but rather clumsy recording gadget.
Burroughs identified his rival's weak spot, went for it,
and devised an excellent printing and tabulating device
which soon became standard on all his machines. But
the market was a booming one, almost impossible to
satiate, and both Burroughs and Felt made fortunes and
launched huge business organizations on the backs of their
ingenuity—the first millionaires of the computer age. The
later application of electrical power to drive the calculators

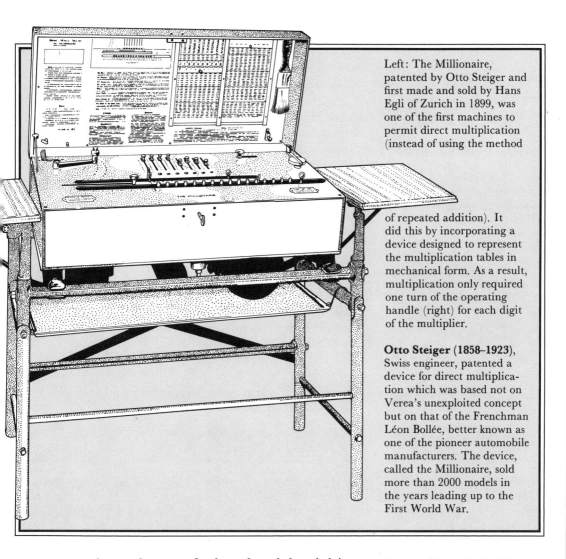

was to open the market even further, though hand-driven
comptometers or Burroughs machines were still doing useful
work in many research laboratories at about the time I
started to work with computers in the early 1960s.

To return now to Hollerith and his triumphant conquest
of the 1890 census. One of the basic features of his success
was that he employed electrical power to drive the tabulating machines. But it is also important to realize that he
made use of electricity in another phase of the automatic
counting, ingeniously bringing it into play in the card-
sorting mechanism itself. The Hollerith cards were, like
the tried and trusted Jacquard cards, stiffish bits of paper
into which holes could be punched at various pre-set
points. The story goes that Hollerith got the idea of coding
personal information about human beings in this way when
he was sitting in a train and watching the conductor punch
holes in passengers' tickets to indicate where they had got
on, whether they were male or female, whether they were
carrying baggage, and so on.

In 1887 Dorr Felt of Chicago invented the Comptometer, one of the world's first key-driven calculating machines.

Felt's first model (below) was a home-made affair, constructed from a wooden macaroni box. Meat skewers were used for keys and rubber bands for springs. Below this is an early production version.

The important innovation is that calculation was performed simply by pressing keys, which actuated the number wheels of a register. No setting of levers, turning of handles or other movement was required. This greatly speeded up the calculation process.

Dorr E. Felt (1862–1930) shared with Burroughs the distinction of launching the business machine era in the 1890s. Felt produced the Comptometer, the first calculating machine to have a full numeric keyboard, and the first practical adding and listing machines. He set up Felt & Tarrant in 1886 to manufacture his inventions. The Comptometer's principal use was for rapid addition and subtraction, and consequently it attracted both business and scientific customers.

The big problem, however, was how to get the machine to read and "interpret" the information punched up on the cards. Jacquard, you will recall, had used a series of rods against which the punched cards were presented at each throw of the shuttle. Some of them slipped through the holes and caused a particular pattern to be woven, while the remainder were stopped in their tracks and had no effect. But in the Hollerith Census machine it was a different kind of information-handling problem, and the operation had to be performed as quickly as possible. Hollerith overcame this by designing his card-reader so that fine rods passed through the holes and dipped into a bowl of mercury, thus completing an electrical circuit which in turn caused a clock to advance by one unit. For each of the possible positions where holes might be punched there existed an appropriate clock, and people were able

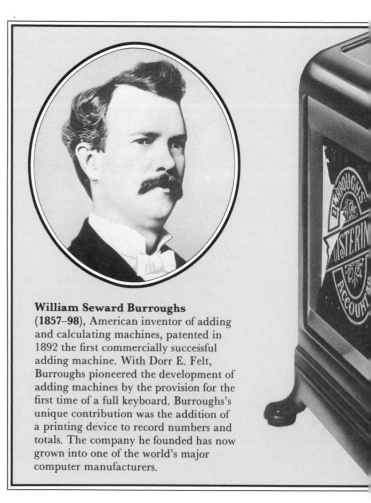

William Seward Burroughs (1857–98), American inventor of adding and calculating machines, patented in 1892 the first commercially successful adding machine. With Dorr E. Felt, Burroughs pioneered the development of adding machines by the provision for the first time of a full keyboard. Burroughs's unique contribution was the addition of a printing device to record numbers and totals. The company he founded has now grown into one of the world's major computer manufacturers.

to sit back in splendour and observe the battery of dials piling up the accumulated data. The reading device was exceedingly fast as electricity doesn't hang around once it has received the go signal, and Hollerith's main difficulty was in devising a system which would move the punched cards across the face of the electrical scanner—for that is what it really was—quickly enough. It was the first hint of a gulf opening up between electrical and mechanical processing systems, and an indication that the days of interlocking cogs and gears were numbered.

The 1890 Census was completed in record time and six weeks after census day it was announced that the popula-

Below: Burroughs's first key-driven adding machine printed rather than displayed results. Depression of the keys denoting the first part of the sum advances a set of number wheels to represent the figures on the keys, and actuates the print mechanism. The keys are then depressed for the second part of the sum, and so on. Depression of the totalizing key causes the result of the sum, stored in the number wheels, to be printed.

tion of the USA stood at 62,622,250. The world sat up and took notice, not so much at the population numbers themselves as at the fact that they had been calculated by machinery—and electrically driven machinery at that. "I am the first statistical engineer," Hollerith declared proudly and correctly, and set up the Tabulating Machine Company in Washington, DC, to handle the rapidly increasing demand for his system.

Among his first big customers were the railways—great compilers of statistics and issuers of accounts and tickets— and the Czarist government of Russia, which, displaying amazing insight for such a feudal bureaucracy, decided to conduct a census using his machines in 1897. Further refinements to the system included improved methods of punching up the cards, quicker methods of sorting, and better methods of coding them so they could carry more

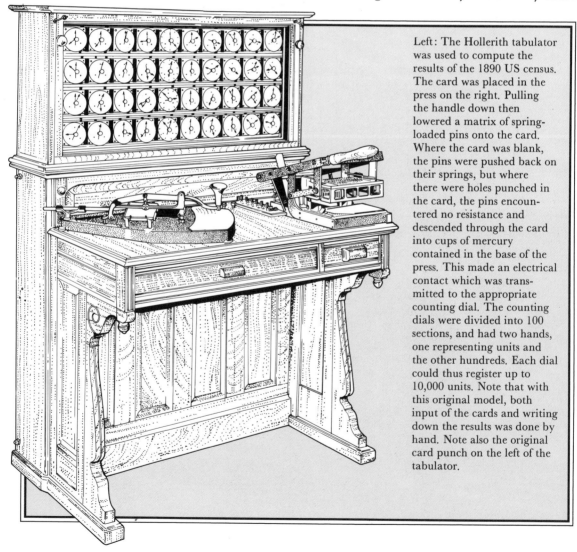

Left: The Hollerith tabulator was used to compute the results of the 1890 US census. The card was placed in the press on the right. Pulling the handle down then lowered a matrix of spring-loaded pins onto the card. Where the card was blank, the pins were pushed back on their springs, but where there were holes punched in the card, the pins encountered no resistance and descended through the card into cups of mercury contained in the base of the press. This made an electrical contact which was transmitted to the appropriate counting dial. The counting dials were divided into 100 sections, and had two hands, one representing units and the other hundreds. Each dial could thus register up to 10,000 units. Note that with this original model, both input of the cards and writing down the results was done by hand. Note also the original card punch on the left of the tabulator.

information. Their size, however, remained standard—Hollerith matched them up, more as a whim than for any other reason, with the dollar bill in circulation at the time, and so they remain to this day. His company went from strength to strength, and in 1911 merged with a number of other time-recording and measuring companies to form a conglomerate known as the Computing Tabulating and Recording Company. Hollerith died at the age of sixty-nine in 1929, while still acting as a consultant to the immense company which he had founded and whose evolution he had partially controlled. By this time it had grown still more and its name was now the International Business Machine Corporation; and today, of course, it is best known as IBM.

We have now reached the point in the narrative where a new concept has to be introduced—the notion of the distinction between two types of approaches to computing, the first employing analogue, the second digital, techniques. It is not really essential to understand the differences between these two in detail to follow the arguments presented in this book, but knowing something about them makes it possible to follow the historical evolution of computers that much better.

The difference between analogue and digital data is most easily conveyed by reference to the two different types of watch. A digital watch tells you the time in digits, for example 4.27. A conventional watch would at the same time show the hour hand half-way between the 4 and the 5, and the minute hand half-way between the 5 and the 6. To generalize, digital data is represented in terms of discrete quantities, each quantity being distinct from the next. Analogue data is represented in terms of points along a scale, each point merging imperceptibly into the next. Neither is better than the other; in fact in the case of our timepieces we would have to translate the data represented in both cases to arrive at the time—"half-past four".

So far all the computing devices mentioned except one have been digital devices, that is they count in distinct units or chunks. The exception is the slide-rule which we mentioned briefly earlier in connection with logarithms. The slide-rule is a static calculator, rather like the abacus in the sense that it does nothing on its own and all the computation is done by the user. But the point about the slide-rule is that it expresses numbers or quantities in terms of distances measured out on its length. To calculate, all you do is tot up the distances representing the numbers in the sum and there is the answer. Now the point is that an analogue device "calculates" by converting the numbers to be dealt with into some physical quantity—distances in

Above: **Herman Hollerith (1860–1929)**, American inventor, was the first to make a practical implementation of punched cards in data processing. The application was the United States census of 1890. It had become clear that processing census results could no longer be done by hand; the growth in population was such that the 1890 results would not have been produced until after the subsequent census in 1900. Hollerith's solution was the use of punched cards, and he developed a series of machines including, notably, the card punch and the tabulator. He formed the Tabulating Machine Company in 1896 to exploit these inventions; the company expanded through a number of acquisitions and mergers and eventually became IBM.

the case of the slide-rule. Other physical quantities can be used. In the case of a crude type of clock such as the egg-timer, time is turned into quantities of sand and its passage is measured by the amount of sand in the upper and lower containers. In the case of measuring heat, one can use simple analogue devices such as columns of mercury, or even bands of metal which expand and contract in proportion to their temperature. In these cases the measure being taken is extremely simple, and we need to step into a higher level of complexity to get an idea how an analogue computer, as opposed to a simple measuring rod, might work. Let us consider the case of electrical currents. It is not difficult to make a device which converts a mechanical movement into electricity and so provide a measure of the amount of movement that has taken place. The wheel in a dynamo, for example, can generate a current which rises proportionally to the number of turns made, and it is easy to see that this current could be fed into a voltmeter, which in turn could cause a needle to move against a scale. And thus one type of measure (distance or engine activity let us say) has been converted into electrical energy—an analogue of the original. If this concept has been grasped, it should be possible to make a conceptual jump to the point where one can accept that quite complex mathematical measures can be set up on analogue machines, particularly, though not exclusively, those employing electrical currents and voltages. For example, many mathematical functions, notably differential equations, can be expressed on paper as a series of curves or cycles. These curves could be converted, inside a machine composed of the appropriate electrical units, into repetitive pulses of electrical energy whose peaks and troughs were proportional to the peaks and troughs of the graph. The integration of sets of these curves—a typical problem in practical mathematics—might be done by putting together matching sets of electrical patterns within the computer. This example is oversimplified, but it gives the essentials of analogue computing in a nutshell. Analogue computers are a bit of a curiosity these days; they are significant, however, in the role they played in the early days of computing. The first successful digital machines were really just number-crunchers, but the first really tough mathematical problems involving the integration of patterns of information (rather than just piling up columns of numbers) were solved by analogue machines. Oddly enough, the very first ones didn't make use of electricity at all and relied on—guess what?—ingeniously organized wheels and gears.

The first really useful analogue computer was built in the 1870s by the British physicist Lord Kelvin, who saw that the integration of two or more variables—as is required in many mathematical problems—can be done by any sets of gears with continuously variable ratios. Anyone who knows anything about the basics of automobile engineering and has considered the ingenious principle of the differential gear which transfers the drive to the two back wheels of most motor cars will have some insight into this fact; others who don't want to bother with the mechanical details might care just to accept it as so. Anyway, Kelvin, aided by a particularly clever "wheel and disc integrator" invented by his brother James Thomson, decided to design an analogue device capable of predicting the tides around the shores of Great Britain. It was a mechanical system of drums, gears, cables, rods and dials, but it worked extremely well and could spell out the times and heights of the ebb and flood tides for any number of years into the future. This, of course, saved an enormous amount of routine computation, and Kelvin tide predictors or variants of them were soon being employed in many countries all over the world. But it was perhaps more important because it showed mathematicians just what a machine could do in the way of computation.

In a remarkable paper published in the *Proceedings of the Royal Society* in 1876, Kelvin indicated that it ought to be possible to build a machine capable not only of dealing with tides but of coping with general problems associated with the solution of differential equations. It was the rough equivalent of Babbage's proposal for a general-purpose Analytical Engine as opposed to his special-purpose Difference Engine. Kelvin coined the term "differential analyser" for his proposed system, and although everyone approved no one did anything about it. Possibly most people were put off at the thought of how large and complex a really multi-purpose differential analyser would be, and the proposal hung fire for almost fifty years. The man to convert it into reality was a brilliant Massachusetts Institute of Technology (MIT) professor who was later to play a potent role in educating the higher echelons of the US Government to the importance of scientific research, both basic and applied. His name was Vannevar Bush, and in considering his work our history jumps into the twentieth century.

Some people consider Bush to be the true father of the computer, and one can make a case to support this view. With a team of young engineers he set out to build a differential analyser, and the first model was finished in 1930. As Kelvin and his contemporaries had guessed, it was very, very big, and it was driven by a bunch of electric motors. Most important of all, it was general-purpose—

Below: Part of Kelvin's tide-predicting machine, a special-purpose analogue computer. Data representing the results of analysis of tidal observations was input via the numbered wheels (of which two out of the 10 are shown). Turning the handle set the machine in motion, and the result, representing a year's tides for a given port, was printed out as a curve on the roll of paper at the front.

William Thomson, 1st Baron Kelvin (1824–1907), Scottish mathematician and physicist, described the principles on which a differential analyser could be built in 1876—a concept developed independently by Vannevar Bush (b. 1890) and his colleagues at MIT in the 1920s. Thomson's work led to the design of a Harmonic Analyser to analyse graphical records of daily changes in atmospheric temperature and pressure; the machine was first used at the Meteorological Office in 1878. Parts of it were built by his elder brother, Professor James Thomson (1822–92), at that time professor of engineering at Glasgow University. William Thomson contributed to research which led to the construction of the first transatlantic cable, for which he was knighted in 1866. He published many papers on electric and magnetic phenomena. His inventions include the mirror galvanometer and the quadrant electrometer.

which is to say that it could, with a bit of reorganization, be set to cope with more or less any problem where differential equations were involved.

This in itself might have been enough to put Bush on the short-list for those with a claim to have invented the computer, but many people feel that he has an even stronger claim. The main components of his analyser were mechanical, and no different in principle from the components of Pascal's first calculator. But Bush was smart enough to realize that these types of components had horrendous limitations, notably in their imperfect tolerances (not fitting together sufficiently precisely, a tendency to mechanical slippage, and so on), in the difficulty of switching them around to solve one type of problem rather than another, and in their achingly slow speed of operation. He decided to take a crucial step and replace some of the mechanical components with thermionic tubes or valves in which the values would be stored as voltages. It was a bold step, but only a partially successful one. The valves were large and unreliable and they consumed an enormous amount of power, which, of course, they also discharged in heat. This meant they had to be spaced widely apart and supplied with coolers, and the analyser grew enormously in size. Nevertheless the beast worked. It was both electronic and general-purpose in nature, and was, unquestionably, the first of its kind.

Can Bush therefore be credited with having been the inventor of the computer? The question highlights the difficulties one gets into when one tries to trace any idea to its source. What, for example, is it claimed that Bush invented? Not the notion of a general-purpose calculating machine—if one has to establish priority then it must be by naming Babbage; nor the notion of a differential analyser, which is clearly spelt out in Kelvin's paper to the Royal Society. In his autobiography Bush claims that he didn't come across the Kelvin paper until after he had built his analyser, which is a little strange, for it is an extremely famous document which had been widely read by engineers. More to the point, perhaps, he adds that ideas are not all that count and the real credit ought to go to those who put their ideas—or even someone else's ideas—into practice. In that case poor old Babbage comes nowhere in the race. But it has to be acknowledged that there is something in Bush's argument. What he did do first was to introduce electronic components into a computing system, and as such the MIT differential analyser represents a turning point in the history of computing.

Vannevar Bush really is a remarkable man and, apart from the differential analyser, he has made significant

contributions to various fields of science. He also had the happy knack of inspiring and fertilizing the minds of bright individuals who came into contact with him. Two British physicists visited MIT in 1933 and gazed in delight at the vast bulk of the differential analyser. They were Douglas Hartree and his student Arthur Porter, and as soon as Hartree saw the array of gears, wheels and rods that made up the equation solver he thought that "someone had been enjoying himself with an extra large Meccano set". Hartree and Porter went back to England and treated themselves to just such a Meccano set, costing all of £20, and out of this they proceeded to build a differential analyser. It was accurate to within about 2% of Bush's monster device, and they used it to solve some quite complex problems in wave mechanics. Later Hartree designed and built a full-scale differential analyser which worked away busily at Manchester University. You can see them both at the Science Museum in London, and while the later analyser is the more impressive physically, my heart is really with the Meccano version—all red and green strips and bright brass gears.

Another brilliant mind which was pushed in precisely the right direction by Bush's guidance was that of Claude Shannon. While a student at MIT he was making a few dollars by operating the differential analyser. The relay

Above: In the MIT differential analyser, built by Vannevar Bush, the central part consists of gears and shafts arranged as required to perform the calculation. When set in motion, they drive the computing parts of the device, known as integrators and contained in cabinets on the right. The boards on the left are used for input and output. Each is equipped with a carriage which can move over the surface of the board in two directions at right angles to each other. For data input, a prepared graph is placed on the board, and the carriage moved so that it follows the curve drawn on the graph. This movement drives the calculating part of the analyser. For output, a pen is fixed to the carriage, and a blank sheet of graph paper placed on the board. The drive is reversed, so that the analyser can transmit the results of its calculations by driving the pen over the graph paper.

Vannevar Bush (b. 1890), American electrical engineer, constructed the first differential analyser with his colleagues at MIT in the late 1920s. In 1940 he was appointed chairman of the National Defense Research Committee, which was responsible for co-ordinating scientific research to help the war effort. In this role he wrote the report recommending the establishment of the Manhattan team, which eventually developed the atomic bomb.

circuits within the analyser were always needing attention, and Bush suggested to Shannon that it ought to be possible to formalize the design of these circuits and to use symbolic logic to do so. Shannon took up the challenge and ultimately came up with his paper, "A Symbolic Analysis of Relay and Switching Circuits", which turned out to be epoch-making. To understand why it was so important we need to resurrect the name of George Boole.

Boole, you may recall, was an English philosopher living around the time of Babbage who showed that the rules and principles of logic were sufficiently well formalized for them to be expressed in mathematical terms. Thus you could use mathematical notation to state logical propositions and, by following the rules of mathematics, follow the various propositions to their ultimate, inescapable conclusions. The link between logic and mathematics had been made, but it had had curiously little impact and sat around in the way that these things sometimes do until somebody turned up who could see how to develop it. The "somebody"—or "somebodies" in this case—who pounced on Boole's great concept were a pair of awesome intellects: Alfred North Whitehead and Bertrand Russell, whose three-volume work *Principia Mathematica* (1910–13) is

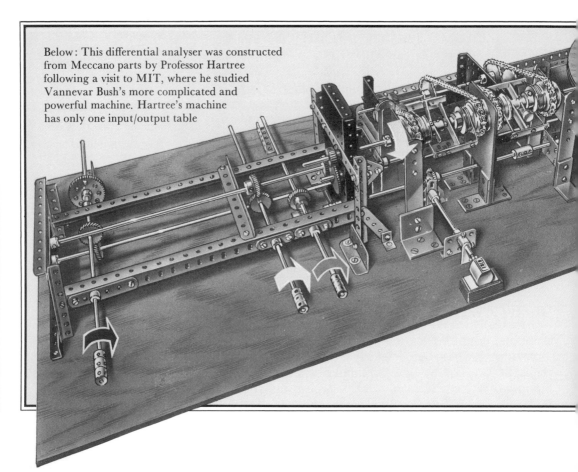

Below: This differential analyser was constructed from Meccano parts by Professor Hartree following a visit to MIT, where he studied Vannevar Bush's more complicated and powerful machine. Hartree's machine has only one input/output table

thought by some people to be one of the most influential scientific texts of all time. In it Whitehead and Russell argued that logic was not only inseparable from mathematics but was also the foundation of it, and they went on to develop a propositional calculus in which problems could be solved in terms of a series of statements that are either true or false. This means that problems other than those of a purely mathematical nature and concerned with matters in the "real world"—"Should I do this or that?" "What happens if?" etc.—can be converted into mathematical form and, in principle at any rate, could be put to a specially programmed computer for solution. The eighteenth-century scientist/statesman the Earl of Stanhope constructed a crude "logic demonstrator" which was a very primitive machine for doing just this.

There had been other developments in the meantime. In the 1880s a logician at Princeton University, Allan Marquand, constructed a machine in which a conclusion could be extracted from a number of premises according to the rules of logic. It was a large wooden box

(centre) and integrator (left of centre). It was driven by a small motor, which was situated at the extreme left. The machine was constructed as a demonstration model to illustrate Hartree's lectures, but was also used for solving simple equations.

Douglas Rayner Hartree (1897–1958), British physicist, was a significant influence in early British computing circles, and was one of the first to use ENIAC as a general-purpose computer. Impressed by the work of Vannevar Bush on differential analysers, he was prompted to build a Meccano version with the aid of a research student, Arthur Porter, at Manchester University in 1935. Manchester subsequently became one of the three leading British centres of computing research and construction after the Second World War; the others were the National Physical Laboratory and Cambridge University, where Hartree was Plummer Professor of Mathematical Physics from 1946 until his death.

Below: **Bertrand Russell, 3rd Earl (1872–1970)**, English philosopher and mathematician,

was one of the greatest logicians of all time. Truly a Renaissance man, his was one of the most widely varied and persistently influential intellects of the twentieth century. For nearly all of his life he had 40 books in print ranging over philosophy, mathematics, science, ethics, sociology, education, history, religion, politics and polemic, and in 1950 he was awarded the Nobel Prize for Literature. His work with his friend and former tutor, Alfred North Whitehead (1862–1947), *Principia Mathematica* (1910–13), demonstrated the indivisible link between logic and mathematics—to the benefit of the development of computers and data processing. Russell was a controversial public figure, married four times, and ardent social reformer: he was an anarchistic left-wing atheist, and was actively opposed in the last three years of his life to the manufacture of H-bombs and the war in Vietnam.

filled up with the familiar assembly of rods, levers, bits of string and pointers, and it could cope with such trivial problems as the following example, chosen from the eccentric mathematician Lewis Carroll's *Symbolic Logic*:

1. No birds, except ostriches, are nine feet high;
2. There are no birds in this aviary that belong to anyone but me;
3. No ostrich lives on mince pies; and
4. I have no birds less than nine feet high.

And what conclusion must one draw from these four premises? Marquand's machine had no difficulty with the problem and would give, in its own way, the conclusion that:

"No bird in this aviary lives on mince pies."

Marquand corresponded with the philosopher Charles Peirce on the subject of logic machines, and this led the latter to make a remarkable suggestion: a simple system of batteries and switches could be put together which would, in principle, be capable of solving quite abstruse problems in formal logic. Peirce sketched out one or two circuits and showed how they would work, but again the idea seems to have been ahead of its time. It was resurrected, however, when Claude Shannon, inspired by Vannevar Bush, reconsidered it fifty years later.

Shannon showed more precisely how one might construct electrical circuits to add, subtract, multiply and so on, and in doing so he also showed that the calculus used for specifying these circuits was effectively identical to the calculus of symbolic logic. At the same time he drew attention, more or less in passing, to a finding which numerous people from Leibniz onwards had flirted with: that for the design of machines to compute numbers, the calculating circuits were greatly simplified when the binary system of counting was employed. In due course Shannon moved on to the Bell Telephone Labs. Here he began to work on the notion that communication and information were aspects of the universe which could be clearly specified, measured and manipulated in much the same way as physical events and states could be measured —a revolutionary thesis which was the starting point of the extremely influential discipline known as Information Theory. Modern computers could not have been developed without making use of the principles of Information Theory, but it is not necessary to go into its extremely advanced concepts in this book. It is enough to note that it exists and that Shannon, guided by Bush, was responsible for starting it off.

Meanwhile, tucked away in another part of the enormous

complex which is Bell Telephone's research headquarters, another young mathematician, George Stibitz, began assembling the circuits for just the kind of thing Shannon had sketched out. Stibitz had not read Shannon's paper and had been working on a problem involving the magnetic circuits of particular telephone relays. On his kitchen table he put together a few experimental circuits powered by dry batteries, and he noticed that one of them, roughly similar to the on/off switch of an electric light, was equivalent to one digit of a binary adder. He immediately drew up a circuit for the "carry" digit, coupled the whole thing up to two small light bulbs to act as "output" and there, on the kitchen table in front of him, was the world's first elementary unit of an electric calculator.

Stibitz soon realized he was on to something. He took his tiny circuit in to his high-powered colleagues at Bell and pointed out that this was the basis of a machine which could cope with any number of binary digits, and thus, in principle, could solve any foreseeable computational problem. Stibitz now drew up a plan for a programmable, or general-purpose, version of the calculator and even though it was never built it is fairly clear from looking at the specifications that it would have worked.

Like many imaginative scientists Stibitz had a touch of the showman about him, and in 1940 he delivered a paper on his computer to the Dartmouth College Mathematical Society. By renting a telephone line back to his computer at Bell he was able to demonstrate the device working remotely—the first time computing had ever been done at a distance and another hint of the shape of things to come. The audience was flabbergasted, and among those present were Norbert Wiener—who is now known as the father of cybernetics—and John Mauchly, who was later to build the world's first fully operational electronic computer, ENIAC. It seems that Stibitz's demonstration and exposition were, literally, eye-openers, and there is a good deal of evidence to suggest they both directed their brains to the concept of digital computing from that moment.

Curiously, although the inherent simplicity of a computer operating on binary rather than decimal arithmetic was spelt out in Shannon's thesis and argued strongly by Stibitz, the very first computers—with one striking exception— were decimal devices. In considering this exception we now turn away from America to the continent of Europe and consider another individual who has been championed as the "inventor" of the computer—and, like Bush, he is a very strong candidate indeed. At the time of writing he is alive and well and living in Germany, and his name is Konrad Zuse.

Above: In the experiment devised in 1952 by Claude Shannon of Bell Laboratories to illustrate the capabilities of telephone relays, an electrical mouse finds its way unerringly through a maze, guided by information "remembered" in the kind of switching relays used in dial telephone systems. Experiments with the mouse stimulated Bell Laboratories in their research for new applications beyond numerical calculation for the logical powers of computers.

Claude Elwood Shannon (b. 1916), American mathematician, joined Bell Telephone Laboratories in 1941 after gaining his PhD at MIT. He made a significant contribution to the branch of mathematics known as information theory by showing how information could be quantified in terms of zeroes and ones and then analysed by strict mathematical methods.

The Spur of War

A hundred years had passed since Babbage abandoned the task of completing his Difference Engine and turned, in what may have been a kind of inspired displacement activity, to dreaming up his general-purpose computer. Suppose that he could have been transported forward in time to look at developments as they had occurred by, say, 1933. Would he have been pleased or disappointed at the way things had developed? He would certainly have been pleased that smallish calculators, which could be looked upon as compact versions of his Difference Engine, were being marketed on a world-wide basis, and that few big businesses or government departments were without them. He would also have been gratified to see the way in which Hollerith had picked up the idea of punched cards for rapid data entry, and fascinated, no doubt, at the use of electricity in both the sorting and driving processes. But he would have been surprised and disappointed at the singular fact that nowhere on earth, despite a century of progress in machine design and construction, and a growing world demand for fast, general-purpose information-processing machines, was there anything that looked at all like a working version of his Analytical Engine. And he would have a right to be surprised and disappointed. The concept and the more or less complete specification of his general-purpose computer were quite comprehensible—Lady Lovelace had worked it through in the 1830s—and engineering skills had by now advanced to the point where it could have been built. In addition, there now existed electrical power, punched card readers, relatively high-speed printers and various other refinements which would have greatly simplified the logistical problems of getting the thing to work. Why then hadn't someone simply taken the Babbage design and at least had a go at building it?

There are two main reasons. The first is that by one of those curious trends of history, Babbage had become an almost completely forgotten figure in the early part of the twentieth century, and was virtually unknown to the generations of engineers who were tinkering with calculators at that time. Secondly, and more importantly, those who did cast their eyes over Babbage's drawings and caught the power of his ideas were also clever enough to realize that a purely mechanical device was simply not on. No matter how well the components were engineered and how carefully they were assembled, the monster contrivance which would have been the inevitable end-product would have been too large, too costly, too unreliable and—above all—too slow to be worth the kind of investment necessary to bring it to the point of birth. The days of the giant cog-and-wheel systems were over and the world was awaiting a shift in the nature of technology before Babbage's dream would be realized. In the 1930s this shift was just beginning to occur. It would take place slowly at first, but then, spurred by one of the most effective forces which promote and harness man's ingenuity—war—it would move with speed, and the era of true computers would arrive.

In the 1930s the threads of the problem were being gathered together, quite independently, by a number of workers in various parts of the world. In the United States, large organizations such as IBM and the Bell Telephone Company were at work. In England the thrust was coming from an individual, the mathematician Alan Turing, whose paper "On Computable Numbers", published in 1936, sent a jolt of enlightenment amongst the cognoscenti. In Germany the threads were in the hands of a young engineer named Konrad Zuse, who had made up his mind not only to design a universal computer but also to build one. As Zuse, unarguably, had the edge in time over all his competitors, we will look at him first.

Zuse was an engineering student at the University of Berlin in Charlottenburg, completing his doctoral thesis at a time when brown shirts and swastikas were enjoying their fleeting vogue throughout Germany. Any latent interest he may have had in the seething politics of the time was totally submerged in his personal obsession, which was to find some way of easing the great computational burden that all design engineers had to bear in the course of their work. Like so many others before him, he considered routine and repetitive calculations to be a scandalous waste of brain power which should as soon as possible be relegated to machines which neither cared nor complained. As a schoolboy he had been interested in automata, and had made a workable change-giving machine out of the German equivalent of a Meccano set and had become impressed at the potential of these kits as practical testbeds for ideas. The same thought, it will be recalled, had occurred to Hartree and Porter when they saw Bush's differential analyser at MIT, and had come back to England to build a simpler version out of Meccano parts. But Zuse knew little about the work going on elsewhere in the world, and certainly had never come across the differential analyser. Had he read about what Hartree and Porter had done with a few simple rods and gears he might well have been tempted to follow their lead and develop something similar. This might or might not have done the job he wanted it to—probably *not*, actually—but he would inevitably have found himself ploughing down the blind alley of analogue machines. Instead he sat back and thought, and he had some very good thoughts indeed.

The first good thought—he claims that he was not aware of Babbage's Analytical Engine—was that one could extend the principles of a special-purpose calculator and build one capable of being programmed to perform *any* mathematical task. His second was that the way to do this was to use binary instead of decimal calculating units, and as he came to this conclusion in 1935 or at the latest 1936, he must have been the first person in the world to do so— and what's more, put the idea into practice. His third thought was that it would be possible to build at least a pilot working model using Meccano parts and cheap "off the shelf" mechanical components.

In 1936, therefore, Zuse announced to his parents, with whom he shared an apartment in Berlin, that he was giving up his bread-and-butter job as a design engineer in order to stay at home and build a computer. His parents, Zuse recalls, were "not very delighted" at the news but took it with the stoicism that the parents of children of genius so frequently seem to have in abundance. Zuse wasted no time. He annexed a table in a corner of their living-room for his rudimentary model, and after a while added another table as the computer grew. Soon more tables and another corner were required, and then the centre of the room surrendered to the machine's advance. Zuse's parents retreated gracefully into the nether regions of the house and provided what financial support they could for the machine, which was now called the Z1. The Z1 was just a testbed, but it was a very successful one and it contained a number of remarkable features. There was, of course, its binary method of operation—and there was the fact that it had a memory and something vaguely equivalent to a central processor. But it also had a keyboard to input the numbers, and a system of electric bulbs to signal the results of the calculation in binary form. It was all enough to tell Zuse that he was on to something, and on to something big.

The next step was to build Z2, which was even more remarkable, and incorporated two radical advances in computer design. In the first place Zuse replaced the Meccano-type mechanical switches, which had constituted the Z1's memory and which he had found were too clumsy and unreliable, with electro-magnetic relays—the kinds of things used in telephone switching gear. This seems to have been the first application of such relays in any computer system. Secondly, he replaced the keyboard input, which was also slow and clumsy and not up to the potential of his machine, with a brilliantly imaginative system roughly equivalent to punched cards or, to be more exact, to punched paper tape. Instead of using tape, which was not available at the time, Zuse used discarded 35 mm film into which were punched the holes which corresponded to the machine's instructions. And lo and behold, when he put all this together, it worked!

And now came a development which might have had enormous consequences not only for the future of computing, but also for the future of mankind, if the right (or perhaps one should say the wrong) men had seen its tremendous potential. In the mid to late 1930s the Germans, like many other people, were movie mad, and one of the most popular movies made in that period was the classic original version of *King Kong*. It will hardly be necessary to outline the plot of *Kong* for any reader, but it is enough to say that Zuse, being a man of taste and culture as well as genius, swiftly recognized it as one of the best films ever made. Many of his friends were of the same opinion, and had gathered themselves together—I suppose you might call it a *King Kong* fan club—to produce a stage version of the story. By any standards it was an ambitious scheme with the climax of the show featuring someone dressed up as King Kong lurching around the stage destroying model elevated trains, smashing down papier mâché skyscrapers and fending off an attack of toy biplanes. Needless to say there was considerable competition in the club for the role of Kong, and Zuse, a large man, might have had every hope that he would have been the lucky one. But there was an even larger youth in the group by the name of Helmut Schreyer, to whom the prized role finally fell. And so, in a series of justly well-attended performances, the saga of King Kong was acted out in an amateur theatre in Berlin, and night after night Herr Schreyer, dressed in a gorilla suit, destroyed a model of the Empire State Building.

And this is where the story really starts. Despite their theatrical rivalry, Zuse and Schreyer became close friends, and the latter, who was looking around for a subject for his doctoral thesis in electrical engineering, showed a sharp interest in Zuse's computers. When Zuse told him he was planning to replace the simple mechanical memory switches with electro-magnetic relays, thus gaining vastly in speed and reliability, Schreyer in a rush of youthful optimism and insight urged him to go one better and use electronic valves or tubes instead. The advantages of electronic components, if suitable circuits could be made with them, would be a huge increase in processing speed. Telephone relays were capable of switching (and thus

Left: **Konrad Zuse** (**b. 1910**), German engineer, had as a child constructed a change-giving machine out of the German brand of Meccano and had noted the potential of such kits as practical testbeds. Zuse started work on program-controlled computing machines in the early 1930s and produced his first product, the Z1, in 1938. The first fully operating machine, the Z3, appeared in 1941. These were electro-mechanical computers. His computer manufacturing company, Zuse AG, was eventually acquired by Siemens in 1969.

Below: The Z1 had keyboard input, used mechanical switches for the storage of numbers and displayed its results via a row of electric light bulbs. A major feature was its use of the binary numbering system. This is a reconstruction of the original, which was destroyed during World War Two.

calculating) five or ten times a second, but valves, if they could be made to work, might operate at the rate of hundreds, even thousands of cycles per second. For a brief period, as they discussed Schreyer's breathtaking idea, there is no doubt that both men were favoured with a glimpse of the future; but inevitably, the realities of the present pressed down on them. Valves were rare, unreliable, extremely expensive and enormous consumers of raw electricity, and the heat they gave off when assembled in sufficient numbers to do any reasonable calculating job would probably cause the rest of the machine to malfunction.

Zuse returned to his relays, and Schreyer went away to think about it more deeply. In 1938 Schreyer was awarded his doctorate in engineering for a thesis which showed how electronic valves could be employed as the basic units for an ultra-high-speed digital computer; but with the coming of the war this thesis found its way on to a library shelf and apparently had no influence whatsoever on the future development of computers. Zuse, after a brief period in the army, worked on engineering problems associated with aircraft design and before long he had interested the Henschel Company in using one of his machines to help speed up the great strings of calculations that are needed to solve the problem of wing flutter in aircraft design. A Z3 and Z4—the latter using a few electronic components— were built, as were a series of special-purpose machines which worked solidly and successfully on problems of aircraft and missile design.

There is another "What if?" question. Suppose some far-sighted individual had connected Schreyer's thesis with Zuse's machines and siphoned, with the implacable dedication that was such a characteristic of the German war effort, large sums of money and effort into constructing a fully electronic computer. What effect might this have had on the course of the war? It has frequently been said that Britain's secret code-cracking computer, which we shall consider later in this chapter, ensured victory for the Allies. Might not the possession of a fully operational machine in German hands at an early stage of the war have had the reverse effect? It is not a particularly pleasant line of thought, but if one pursues it one comes to the conclusion that the consequences would not have been all that disastrous, mainly because the peculiarly blinkered philosophy of the German war effort prevented this happening. By 1940 Hitler was convinced that Germany had all but won the war, and he directed that all scientific research in connection with warlike goals should be of short duration only. So in 1940, when Zuse and Schreyer formally put to the authorities the very considerable potential of high-speed computers for code-cracking, they were asked if it would take longer than a year to build one. They had to admit that it would, whereupon the project was dismissed immediately as being likely to reach fruition only after the date at which the war would have been won.

But the war didn't end to Hitler's timetable, and most of Zuse's machines met a fiery death in Berlin in 1944. He did, however, manage to rescue his last one, the Z4, and in the rather crazy closing months of the conflict traipsed south across Germany, in the company of Wernher von Braun, hoping to achieve the twin goals of saving his invention and avoiding capture by the Russians. Somehow or other he reached the Alps and found a remote village; he hid the Z4 in a cellar and tried to maintain a low profile, while his fertile brain churned away on the idea of a universal programming language for the computers of the future. All might have been well had the villagers not become suspicious about the weird contrivance he was hiding amongst the apple barrels, and formed the conclusion that this just had to be the last of Hitler's secret weapons. Before long the Allied authorities got curious and annexed Zuse and his computer. He was briefly interned and questioned but, as he was in no way implicated in war crimes, was released and later went on to form a successful computer company which was in due course swallowed up by Siemens. Today he is a retired businessman living in Germany who has found himself a place in history. His friend Schreyer drifted off to South America after the war, and also became successful in business. From time to time he flies over to Europe to see Zuse and the two meet to talk about things, including computers, old friends and—I have no doubt—*King Kong*.

At about the time Zuse was completing the Z1 in his parents' front room on a budget which had to be scratched together on a daily basis, an attempt, on a much grander scale and with the massive resources of IBM behind it, was being made in the United States to construct a general-purpose computer using magnetic relays. The originator of the idea was a young associate professor of mathematics at Harvard, Howard H. Aiken. Comparing the two projects—Zuse's and Aiken's—is almost impossible because of the chasm-like difference in scope and financial backing. Just about the only thing in common between them was the fact that they were both pushed along by men of iron will and an unquestioned faith in their capacity to chew and digest everything they could get their teeth into. But the most interesting separation point is that whereas Zuse was working more or less from scratch, designing a machine which—so far as he knew—had never even been thought of before, Aiken was consciously and deliberately setting out to construct, using the technology of the moment, a modern equivalent of Babbage's Analytical Engine. Thus, though Zuse undoubtedly had a working system operating before the war and Aiken's giant system didn't start working in earnest until 1943, it is the latter system that is generally accepted as having been the first to fulfil Babbage's dream.

The story of the construction of what came to be known as the Harvard Mark I computer starts from a familiar platform—its inventor's concern at the huge amount of time and effort which human beings had to expend in performing the endless calculations which science, technology and government were generating.

In 1936, after reading Babbage's original works thoughtfully, Aiken began to wonder whether it might be possible to combine into one unit a collection of the more effective calculating machines of the time, and in particular the highly successful 601 Multipliers manufactured by the IBM Company. It didn't take him long to realize that a lash-up of special-purpose machines would be a complete waste of time, and that the only way to achieve a general-purpose calculator would be to start from the ground up; equally apparent to him was the fact that a project of this kind would need considerable technical resources and back-up and, most of all, lots and lots of money. But it was also obvious that given these useful things, an Analytical Engine, mid-twentieth-century style, could be made to work.

IBM was already a highly successful company. It had made enormous sums out of selling calculators and might be expected to be interested in making more out of the calculators of the future. It was an obvious possibility for a touch. It was run by Thomas J. Watson, a cranky autocrat who frequently acted on hunch and who could either sink or float a project with one word. Aiken did his homework and consulted one of IBM's most respected employees, James Bryce, who had coughed up about four hundred useful inventions for IBM in the thirty years he had been with the company and was believed to have Watson's ear as much as any man had. Bryce quickly saw the force of Aiken's plan, spoke to his boss about it and, true to form, Watson made an instant binary decision and handed over a million dollars just like that. At this moment the war came and made Aiken a Navy lieutenant, but when it was obvious that his computer would be tailor-made to solve naval problems he was released on detachment to complete the job. There was a lot of hard work, but surprisingly few big snags. Aiken had opted, correctly, for a digital rather than an analogue computer, and had decided that its basic unit should be electro-magnetic relays. He seems never to have considered valves seriously, arguing that their vast superiority in speed would be easily outweighed by their unreliability—better a slow-working machine than a fast inoperative one. The main design and creative work took place at Harvard, but the assembly of the system was done at IBM's headquarters at Endicott, where it was first switched on briefly in 1943. It was then pulled apart for modifications and partial redesign and reassembled in the physics labs at Harvard.

Anyone coming up against the Harvard Mark I, as it was called, tended to gape in amazement. It was a monster, fifty-five feet long, eight feet high and containing not much less than a million individual components. Nothing like it had ever been built before, and nothing like it would ever be built again. At Watson's insistence, it had been decked out in "streamlined" stainless steel and glass, as befitting the image of what he considered an IBM product of this kind should be. The effect was truly mind-blowing, and although it was really an intellectual brontosaurus to those who knew what computers might very shortly be able to do, it corresponded in visual terms with the public's image of the science-fiction world of the future. To add to the sense of clinical perfection, it was staffed and run by engineers who had been drafted into the Navy along with Aiken. They were expected to behave like Navy personnel and marched smartly back and forth across the polished floor saluting each other and, according to a contemporary scientist from Harvard, who despite his scruffy appearance was once allowed in to have a peep, "appearing to operate the thing while at attention".

The Mark I received enormous amounts of publicity, particularly when the war ended and security wraps came off. Glossy magazines carried detailed pictures of its glittering façade, and the dread phrase "electronic brain" appeared in print for the first time. For all its pretensions it was an extremely slow device—the generation of computers which came into being only a year or so later were well over a thousand times faster—and it was also noisy in a way that no other computer has ever been. As one stood in reverence on its polished floor one could hear relays clicking away as the numbers churned laboriously around its innards—a sound described in someone's memorable phrase as "like listening to a roomful of old ladies knitting

Thomas J. Watson, senior (1874–1956), American, has assumed legendary proportions within the computer industry, partly because of his autocratic rule over IBM for more than 40 years and partly because of the success of William Rodgers's best-seller, *Think*. Watson made his name with NCR as a salesman of cash registers, and it was there that he originated his famous instruction, "Think". He left NCR in 1913 to become president of the Computing Tabulating and Recording Company, a punched card equipment manufacturer, which, by introducing the selling methods successful with cash registers, he transformed into the leading manufacturer of business machines. The company was renamed International Business Machines in 1924. Watson remained in charge of IBM until he handed over to his eldest son, Thomas John junior, shortly before his death. His success derived from his aggressive selling methods, which were highly controversial and landed him in legal trouble both with NCR and IBM. His two sons both held senior executive positions within IBM and both became US ambassadors, Thomas John to Moscow and the younger son, Arthur Kitteridge, to Paris.

away with steel needles''.

It did have one big effect, and that was to place the name of IBM in the forefront of computer manufacture, and mindful of this, perhaps, Watson produced the very considerable backing necessary to build a Mark II model, despite the fact that he had fallen out bitterly with Aiken over the details of the Mark I commissioning ceremony. But technology was whipping along, and experiments with fully electronic computers which had been going on in some secrecy in the USA—and in crushing secrecy in the UK—had rendered the Mark II obsolete before it was completed.

The British effort in the early days of the true computers was a very considerable one. It arose partly because of the country's tradition of excellence in mathematics and electrical and communication engineering, and partly because of the pressing needs of a war which had, in the early days of 1940, reached a point where the nation's survival was genuinely threatened. Europe was firmly squashed under Hitler's feet and an invasion of Britain was a real possibility. In the meanwhile America was detached and able to pursue the development of computers at a pace which was determined more by business than by emergency

Below: The Harvard Mark I was the first successful attempt to construct a machine with the capability of Babbage's Analytical Engine. It was sponsored by IBM.

Left: **Howard Hathaway Aiken** (1900–73), American computer pioneer, was struck by the need to improve the power of computational aids. At Harvard University he conceived the idea of an immense calculator, using electro-mechanical relays and controlled by instructions fed in on paper tape. Its cost was too high for the University to bear, but IBM eventually agreed to back the project. Initially called the Automatic Sequence Controlled Calculator (ASCC) but now more usually known as the Harvard Mark I, it was built at the IBM Development Laboratories at Endicott and completed in 1943. Addition or subtraction of two numbers took three-tenths of a second; it was the first fully automatic computer to be built and remained in use at Harvard night and day for about 15 years. Aiken was an irascible man and refused to acknowledge Watson's role in the project.

requirements. In military terms Britain could forget any idea of competing with Germany as an equal, and her only chance was to use her wits to bluff and outsmart the enemy until such time as the military balance could be redressed. In particular, her need was to keep one jump ahead of her opponent's moves by penetrative military intelligence. For decades almost all diplomatic and military exchanges had been conducted in codes, and as one code was cracked so more elaborate ones went out in its place. The science of code-making and code-breaking—cryptography—evolved steadily as a result, and before long machines were being used actually to create codes, which meant they could be changed from day to day. The story of how the Polish secret service captured the German's newest code machine, Enigma, and shipped it back to England has been told on a number of occasions, but what is perhaps less well known is that Enigma's secrets were themselves revealed with the help of the world's first working electronic computer. The site of this triumph was a country house in Hertfordshire known as Bletchley Park.

Only sketchy details are available because much of the work at Bletchley is still classified information and blanketed by the Official Secrets Act. At an early stage of the war the British Government began recruiting a team of all-aces mathematicians and electronics experts; they closeted them away at Bletchley and ordered them to work out how machines could best be employed in tackling crypto-analysis. It is clear that someone at a high level had decided that machines, electro-mechanical or electronic in nature, should be employed in tackling some aspects of crypto-analysis, but who was responsible for this important executive decision is not known. The first approach was to use electro-magnetic machines with telephone-type relays of the kind that went into Aiken's and Zuse's devices. One of the main people involved in the design was the interesting figure of Alan Turing, whose paper "On Computable Numbers" is considered by some to be at least as significant as Shannon's later work.

There was a series of electro-magnetic machines and they had joky British nicknames like the "Heath Robinson" after the 1930s cartoonist (roughly equivalent to the American Rube Goldberg), who drew bizarre working models of things like steam-driven mousetraps. Later versions included the "Peter Robinson" and the "Robinson and Cleaver", both called after London stores, and, finally, the "Super Robinson". The remarkable thing about these machines, apart from the fact that they cracked codes, was that they were fed their information on punched paper tape, which passed through a photo-electric reader capable of scanning characters at the rate of two thousand per second. Such a stupendous rate of absorbing data was totally unheard of at the time, and is pretty remarkable even today. So fast was the tape pulled through the reader that it would rise into the air in a series of loops which would hold their position like peculiar aerial sculptures, although the tape was moving at such speed that it would have been dangerous to touch it. This high rate of input merited a high rate of computing, and the team moved on from the Robinson series, which employed relatively slow relays, to the so-called Colossus series, which employed valves as their basic units. Some amazing people were roped in to work on these, all under the leadership of an outstanding mathematician and administrator, Professor Max Newman. Others in the cast included the chief engineers, T. H. Flowers and A. W. M. Coombs; two brilliant mathematicians, I. J. Good and D. Michie; and in the background, moving from project to project as required, the seminal figure of Turing.

Pictures of Colossus—the first one was installed and operating in December 1943—are hard to come by, but it looks like something that's been put together in a real hurry. There is no sign of stainless steel or plate glass; nor was there much saluting and standing to attention, one suspects. All the computing was done by valves, two thousand of them in all (an unheard-of number at the time), and to feed their guzzling appetite for information the paper tape input was pushed up somehow to five thousand characters per second. Many people think Colossus won the war for the Allies. The Germans, confident that their Enigma Machine would produce uncrackable codes, used it in blissful complacency throughout the war, believing their telecommunication messages to be inviolate. And who can blame them? No one, with the exception of the select and silent few who were hatching it out in the rambling country house at Bletchley, could have anticipated the tremendous power of the computer once it began to work or how swiftly and surely it would make its first dramatic mark. And even they, it seems, were taken by surprise at its achievements.

One day, perhaps, those who worked at Bletchley will be released from the bonds of secrecy that now keep them silent, and another chapter, perhaps a crucial one, will be added to the fascinating history of computers. It is no secret, however, that the brilliant team were all conscious of the very great significance of the project they were working on, and most had at least a glimmer of an understanding of the fact that Colossus was but the first step in a giant evolutionary process, and that its capacity, speed and information-processing powers were as nothing in comparison with what its successors would achieve. This realization, it seems, came more easily to the "thinkers" in the team—mathematicians like Good, Michie and Turing—than to the "doers"—the engineers like Flowers and Coombs. The latter had the job of building the thing and making it work, while the others could indulge in the occasional luxury of speculating about what they were getting themselves into. In particular their thoughts drifted to the eerie topic of the relationship between information-processing, which was what Colossus could do, and the nature of human intelligence, thought and reasoning. Significantly they were all united in the view that the real importance of their work was not so much that they were cracking the German military cipher machine, but rather that they were pioneers in the wild and woolly field of machine intelligence. In later years Turing was to write some remarkable papers on machine thought, reasoning and consciousness, and both Michie and Good have moved on to become major figures in this same field.

Once the first Colossus had been built and had demonstrated its worth, the construction of others proceeded at breakneck speed, and ten were built and installed before the war ended. They were, without question, the world's first electronic digital computers, and their performance

Right: The first successful electronic computer was Colossus 1, which started work in December 1943. It was a special-purpose device designed to help the cryptanalysis experts at Bletchley Park during World War Two.

in terms of speed of computation was staggeringly in advance of any mechanical or electro-mechanical device, including the Harvard Mark I, which at that time had just been completed in America. But they were special-purpose machines, dedicated to the task of code-cracking and not modifiable, without very considerable difficulty, to tackle any other problem. Thus they were not a realization of Babbage's Analytical Engine, to which the Aiken machine was much closer in spirit.

The three computers we have talked about in this chapter, the Zuse machines, the Harvard Mark I and Colossus, were to a large extent the children of war, and all of them were to have an influence on the progress of the war—the Colossus in particular, the Zuse and Aiken machines to a lesser degree. Government and military pressures persisted after the termination of hostilities, and machines that had been conceived during the later stages of the war but had never computed a number in anger continued to receive government funding to ensure their completion and further evolution. The most important and successful of these was the machine built at the Moore School of Engineering in Pennsylvania, and installed at the Aberdeen weapons proving grounds in Maryland in 1946. It has the long-winded name of Electronic Numerical Integrator and Calculator, which shortened down nicely to the acronym ENIAC, and it was the machine which ushered in the computer age.

Left: **Alan Mathison Turing (1912–54)**, English mathematician and logician, was one of the most influential figures in the development of the electronic computer. He earned his PhD at Cambridge and published what is generally agreed to be one of the most important single papers in the foundations of computer science, "On Computable Numbers", in 1936. He specified in this a theoretical computer which is infallible and has infinite data storage—the Turing machine. As a young mathematician, he was recruited for the Bletchley Park team during World War Two and is credited with a vital role in the development of the Colossus code-breaking computer, now accepted as the first operational electronic computer. In 1945 he started work on the construction of the Pilot ACE computer at England's National Physical Laboratory and in 1948 joined the group developing computers at Manchester University, where he remained until his early death.

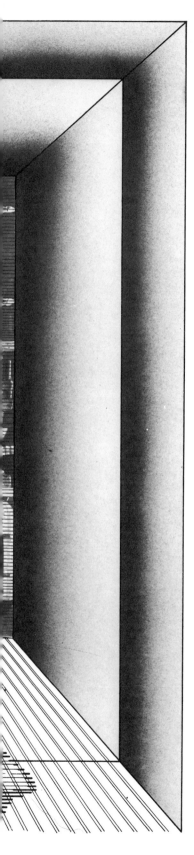

Faster than Thought

The three successful attempts at developing working computers which we covered in the last chapter were pursued quite independently in three different countries, and under conditions which varied from secret to ultra-secret. The only links between the projects were through the small pool of common knowledge about what had already been done with automatic calculation and what could, in principle, be done. The varied choice of technology highlights the independence of the work. Aiken believed in electromagnetic relays and had a deep-seated distrust of electronic components. Zuse would have liked to have gone for electronic components, but could not get the financial support to employ them, and contented himself with a working relay machine. The British at Bletchley, perhaps because of the peculiar nature of their task which screamed out for the highest possible processing speeds, took a jump into the dark and went for an electronic system—and, as we know, they landed firmly on their feet.

The conditions of secrecy which had prevailed in the early forties began to relax after the end of the war. Members of the various research teams visited each other, and returned home carrying with them any choice items they had gleaned. Pockets of secrecy remained, of course: the programs which were being developed at Los Alamos for the hydrogen bomb weren't passed around with the beer and sandwiches, and companies like IBM and the Rand Corporation, who were beginning to flex their muscles in anticipation of post-war commercial competition, kept tight wraps on their design plans. But there was a certain amount of cross-fertilization, and it helped to push things along quite considerably.

The Moore School project began as a top secret military effort. Its goal was to develop an extremely rapid machine capable of rattling off the thousands of computations necessary for compiling ballistic tables for new guns and missiles. Calculating these tables by hand was a maddeningly slow and labour-intensive task, and in the 1940s the military had found themselves in the embarrassing position of having new weapons ready to go into service long before their performance had been properly computed. At the Moore School of Electrical Engineering the problem was put to Dr John Mauchly, who, it will be recalled, had been an extremely interested member of the audience to which, in 1940, Stibitz had demonstrated his simple electronic switching circuit.

At first, Mauchly considered the possibility of an analogue machine. He was familiar with Bush's differential analyser (which had been doing its not particularly marvellous best to help with ballistic tables), but he realized that there were formidable, possibly insurmountable, problems in squeezing much more out of that kind of computer. A digital machine was clearly a must, and in Mauchly's view it ought to be an electronic one. Also at the Moore School was a twenty-two-year-old engineer by the name of J. Presper Eckert, who not only shared his conviction that the only way to tackle the problem was by harnessing the immense switching speeds of electronic valves, but who also had a few clever ideas about how a big valve system might be made to work. Together they put forward a proposal, in August 1942, featuring a detailed design specification for such a machine and federal funding to the extent of $400,000 was approved.

They faced new and taxing problems, not the least of which was that no one had any experience of a machine of any kind—let alone a computer—employing more than a few hundred valves. Needless to say they had no access to the information and experience of the Bletchley team in England, and indeed were not even aware of its existence. Nevertheless they pressed on, and after a twenty-four-hour-a-day programme stretching over thirty months, their Electronic Numerical Integrator and Calculator, ENIAC, was finally assembled and switched on in February 1946. It worked on the decimal rather than the binary system, and it had almost all the characteristics of today's big computers—with one exception, which we will touch on shortly. It was massive, as were all the early computers, filling up a huge room, and it had the unheard-of number of eighteen thousand valves, or tubes as they are known in America. The electricity to supply all these would have kept a small power station busy, and the heat generated by them posed awful cooling problems. Nevertheless ENIAC worked, and it worked at very great speed.

At a special public demonstration in 1946, when the press were shown what was then believed to be the world's first and only electronic computer (Colossus was still wrapped up in secrecy), the machine was set to multiply the number 97,367 by itself five thousand times and a reporter pushed the button to make it do so. The machine completed what, to all the naïve humans present, must have seemed like an impossible task in less than half a second, leading one newspaperman to describe ENIAC's operations as being "faster than thought". And indeed, if one takes switching or processing speeds as the criterion, then ENIAC had jumped way ahead of the equivalent speeds in the human brain, whose neurones switch at a pathetic hundred cycles per second. ENIAC was operating at the conservative rate of tens of *thousands* per second, and the gulf between man as a routine number-cruncher and the machines he had created immediately became unbridgeable.

ENIAC could now get down to work in earnest generating ballistic tables and weather forecasts, which it did with the occasional hiccup as valves—which have a rather high failure rate—winked out from time to time. Its limitations, however, were already clear to Eckert and Mauchly. In particular it had a ludicrously tiny memory for such a giant machine. More important, while programmable in principle (unlike Colossus) it was only capable of being switched from one kind of task to another with great difficulty. To change a program, one literally had to rewire part of the machine.

The problems might have taken a good deal longer to solve than they did had it not been for a chance meeting that had taken place between two of the most significant figures in the field. While waiting for a train on the Aberdeen (Maryland) station in 1945, one of the ENIAC team, Herman Goldstine, bumped into the world-famous mathematician John Von Neumann. Both men had very high security clearances and they were able to while away the time by discussing various aspects of each other's problems. Von Neumann was working on the design of nuclear weapons, and felt handicapped by the advanced mathematics involved because of the delays in the routine checking of his calculations. When Goldstine told him about the very high speeds it was hoped to achieve with ENIAC, his ears pricked up, and from that moment on he became increasingly interested in the project. He never used ENIAC in the basic computations for the atom bomb—the test model was exploded almost two years before ENIAC was commissioned—but he did turn a part of his vastly superior mind to general problems of computation. Part of the reason for this, no doubt, was that he was already engaged in considering the hydrogen bomb and hoped that computers would help in its design—as indeed they ultimately did. But a more important reason was that his exceptional brain was fired by the immense possibilities of computers, which he had already identified as being far more interesting and more important to mankind than thermonuclear weapons.

The result of that chance meeting was that in 1946 Von Neumann eagerly came in as a special consultant to the Moore team, who were then beginning to work on their new computer, EDVAC, and he brought with him the vital

Right: **John Presper Eckert (b. 1919)** and **John William Mauchly** (1907–80) are the two Americans credited with the invention of ENIAC, which although primarily designed to calculate trajectories of bombs and shells during World War Two became the world's first general-purpose electronic digital computer. Eckert and Mauchly were scholars at the Moore School of Electrical Engineering at the University of Pennsylvania, and they conceived the idea of building a calculator using thermionic valves rather than electro-mechanical relays (as Aiken was doing), a technical advance which resulted in a thousand-fold increase in calculating speed. The idea was taken up by the US Army Ordnance Corps, and work on what was to be ENIAC started in 1943, though it was not completed until after the war in 1946. Eckert and Mauchly developed the concept to produce the EDVAC design, but before this was completed they left the University to set up their own company, the first devoted to building and selling computers. It was this company (later taken over by Remington Rand) which produced UNIVAC I.

Below: ENIAC was an enormous device using 18,000 radio valves and thus considerable electrical power. Although removal of the resultant heat represented a serious problem, as did the dubious reliability of the valves, ENIAC was used for 10 years and triggered the postwar computer boom. It was designed to calculate ballistic trajectories, but could be adapted, albeit with considerable labour, to perform any calculation.

concept of the stored program. This is the component which divides every computer, up to and including ENIAC, from all later systems, great and small. The development of the stored program is the major single factor which allowed computers to advance way beyond the power of ENIAC and its various contemporaries. It is also a concept which is of fundamental importance.

At the risk of alienating readers who have some knowledge or understanding of computers, it is essential at this point to recap a bit. A computer is a device for handling or processing information—permuting it if you like—in some way that is useful to human beings. Mostly this is to do with numbers, because so much of the information that needs processing in our increasingly complicated world is numerical. But the notion that computing is *only* to do with numbers is a misleading one, though it blinkered many of the early designers, users and manufacturers of computer systems. Numbers are themselves only concepts which have been coded for our convenience. Furthermore when they are fed into computers they are themselves coded yet again into whatever form the machine likes to work with—in the case of most computers today it is a series of binary switches of some kind. Equally, letters and words are merely coded concepts and they too can easily be recoded so the computer can handle them.

When we get right down to it, all we have, in terms of the basic working components of the computer, is a series— possibly an immense series—of switching units, and you could say that the power of the computer is measured in terms of the number of these units, and the speed at which they can be switched. And is that all that makes a computer powerful? The answer is No. A computer can be said to be powerful not only in terms of its capacity and its speed but also in terms of how many different things it can do which employ its capacity and speed. By this token Colossus was a powerful computer on two counts—speed and capacity—but an exceedingly weak one on the third, for it could only do one thing: crack codes. ENIAC was more powerful on all three counts, being slightly faster, having a much bigger capacity and also being capable, with a bit of effort, of switching from one task to another. With this third factor we are talking about a computer's "programmability".

This is not quite as straightforward as it seems, for when we speak of a computer's programmability, we might be talking either about how easy it was to change its programs—virtually impossible without rebuilding in the case of Colossus, and possible but awkward in the case of ENIAC—or how many and how effective were the

Herman H. Goldstine (b. 1913), American, served in World War Two as a lieutenant in the US Army, where he was responsible for organizing calculations of ballistic trajectories. This was done by using differential analysers, and was therefore greedy of man-hours. Goldstine came across the work of Eckert and Mauchly and realized that their ideas could solve his problem: and thus the US Army Ordnance Corps provided the impetus that led to the development of ENIAC.

Johann von Neumann (1903–57), Hungarian-born mathematician, is usually known as John von Neumann. He escaped from Hungary in 1919, studied chemistry at Berlin, chemical engineering at Zurich, mathematics at Budapest and on a Rockefeller fellowship met the nuclear physicist Oppenheimer at Gottingen. In the States, he worked on the ENIAC project and subsequently embarked on his own programme of theoretical research, which led in 1946 to the production of a paper, with two colleagues, called "preliminary discussion of the logical design of an electronic computing instrument", which was to be extremely influential in all subsequent computer design. Noteworthy was his recognition that program instructions can be treated as numbers and stored in the same way as data. The paper suggested that about 1000 words could be stored, which was 50 times ENIAC's capacity; today's computers can store from 10,000 up to millions. Von Neumann worked on the atomic bomb project during World War Two, and giant computers such as MANIAC (a label donated by Von Neumann himself) were constructed on the basis of his mathematical work for high-speed calculations for H-bomb development.

programs that had been written for it. Anyway a general-purpose computer, as Babbage realized and as Turing proved mathematically, is capable, in principle, of *limitless* flexibility in the way it processes information. In practice the limits of the flexibility are determined by the ingenuity of the person who programs it.

Now let us return to ENIAC as it was when Von Neumann began to think about it, and see how he might have gone about trying to make it more powerful. Assuming he couldn't do anything about its speed or capacity, then the only solution would be to tackle its flexibility. The first thing would be to write some more programs for it—say programs specifically to deal with hydrogen bomb equations. ENIAC would now be a more powerful system, and if Von Neumann had wanted to, he could have made it even more powerful by writing more programs, and soon he would have a whole suite of them. But then a horrible limitation of ENIAC would emerge. Although, in principle, the system was now capable of doing lots of different things, its usefulness would be greatly cut down because of the difficulty of switching from one program to another. One solution might be to devise a system for feeding programs into it more rapidly—by using punched paper tape or whatever. Another solution, and it was here that the lamp of genius flickered in Von Neumann's head, would be to *store the programs within the computer itself.*

This resulted in two immediate and very great gains. In the first place, one could take advantage of the computer's huge processing speed and allow *it* to change programs when required; it could switch from one program to another in a fraction of a second, instead of relying on the lumbering skills of its attendant human being. In the second place, and this is far and away the most important point, it meant that programs within the system could effectively interlock and interact. Programs could call up other programs, switching back and forth as required. In principle, programs could even *modify* other programs, rewriting them to fit the needs of the moment and integrating them with yet others within the suite. From this moment on, computers were no longer fast but blinkered workhorses, woodenly proceeding down one track and one track only, but had become dynamic, flexible information-processing systems capable of performing multitudes of different tasks.

In one conceptual jump, the true power of computers moved from the finite to the potentially infinite. Once Von Neumann's concept had been worked through in the minds of the Moore School team, no one had any doubt that their next model, EDVAC, would have to be a stored program computer and indeed that every computer built from that moment on would have to be based on Von Neumann's invention. And so it turned out to be.

In the interest of putting over the point about why and how stored programs are so important to the history and evolution of computers, I have made the unhesitating assertion that the idea was Von Neumann's and his alone. He is certainly the strongest candidate, but, as is so often the case, it is extremely difficult to trace a fresh idea to its source. Some people credit Eckert with the idea, some Mauchly and some even Alan Turing—who is known to have had a number of lengthy and important meetings with Von Neumann when he visited the USA on hush-hush business during the war. But what really matters is that the stored program came about, and computers moved on an evolutionary step.

Ironically, although everyone beavered away like mad at the Moore School, and despite the massive talents available to them, when EDVAC came into operation it was not the first computer in the world to incorporate a stored program. This very considerable honour would seem to go to the first of a series of pioneering computer systems constructed under the leadership of Professor Tom Kilburn and the late Sir Freddy Williams at Manchester University. This machine, usually called the Mark I, executed its first program in 1948, as reported in a short letter to the British journal *Nature* entitled "Electronic Digital Computers". As this small system was best known as a testbed for a remarkable new approach to computer memory which Williams had invented, its claim to fame in this respect has often been overlooked in favour of the EDSAC machine. This was built at Cambridge University by an energetic team led by Maurice Wilkes, who had clearly been keeping his eyes and ears wide open when he attended lectures at the Moore School in 1946. EDSAC ran its first stored program in May 1949, almost two years ahead of EDVAC.

And now the pace really began to hot up. In the United States big business began to stir the pot as IBM, Bell Telephone and Sperry-Rand started to design computers for the market-place. At first, Bell built some interesting machines, but never really attempted commercial competition; and Rand, who led in the early days, gradually found themselves being displaced by the ruthless marketing strategies of IBM, which was still run by the martinet Thomas J. Watson. In Britain, which briefly held a world lead in computing science, powerful computers appeared at Manchester University, at Cambridge under Wilkes, and at the National Physical Laboratory, where A. M. Turing worked for a period on the design of ACE—at one

Above: The suitability of the computer for administrative work, as opposed to rapid calculation, was first recognized by the Lyons Teashop Company, which in 1949, after two years' planning, recruited John Pinkerton (b. 1919) to design a business computer called LEO. LEO performed its first jobs in 1951 though regular weekly data processing did not start until January 1954. The delay was due to the difficulty in getting the input and output devices to work fast enough. This problem did not affect the other early computers as their prime function was complex calculations which require minimal data input and output. Lyons established a separate company to market LEO computers and this is now part of ICL. Dr Pinkerton still works for ICL today and was involved in the design of ICL's latest range of computer systems.

Above: **Professor Tom Kilburn (b. 1921)** and **Sir Frederick Calland Williams (b. 1911)** were the leaders of the Manchester University team that produced the first alterable store program computer to become operational—in 1948—and established the University as a major centre of computer research, a position it has maintained ever since. Williams (right) was professor of electrical engineering at the University at the time, and Kilburn (left), his junior, became the first professor of computer science anywhere in England in 1964.

Below: The Manchester University Mark I ran its first program in 1948, and is therefore usually credited as the world's first alterable store program computer. The machine was notable for its use of a new type of direct access memory system (Williams tube), and was the first of the University's pioneering computer systems.

time the most advanced and powerful computer in the world. In Britain, too, there was a pioneering use of computers by the giant food corporation, Lyons, which set about constructing its own system, LEO, and a number of British firms, building on the expertise of the war years, dipped into the expanding market. But although the pace in the USA was marginally slower at first, the vast springs of the American economy and the huge sums of money which could be ploughed into computing soon began to pay off. Computers, often built to military requirements, appeared all over the USA and in the early fifties IBM began to market some small business machines.

Costs, however, were still enormous and components unreliable, and it was universally assumed that computers, while doing wonders for the kinds of organizations that required massive and costly routine calculations, would never, *could* never, play any meaningful role in the lives of ordinary people. They were too big, too expensive to buy, too difficult to maintain and service, and far, far too complicated for the average person to understand. In other words, computers seemed to be settling down in the kind of role which other highly specialized pieces of technology—submarines, cyclotrons or power stations—played in the life of the world at large. They were useful, impressive and powerful, but there could never really be many of them. And then, suddenly, from one of the brightest brains at Bell Telephone Labs, came the invention of the transistor. And with it computers moved rapidly from the past and into the present.

Maurice Vincent Wilkes (b. 1913), Dr and now Professor and English computer scientist, worked with the ENIAC team at Pennsylvania in 1946 and then returned to England to head a team at Cambridge University which designed EDSAC (Electronic Delay Storage Automatic Calculator). EDSAC was influenced by EDVAC, but in fact preceded it into operation, executing its first program in May 1949. EDSAC itself inspired LEO, the first business computer. Wilkes was elected a Fellow of the Royal Society in 1956, and was the first president of the British Computer Society (1957–60). He is currently Head of the Computer Laboratory at Cambridge.

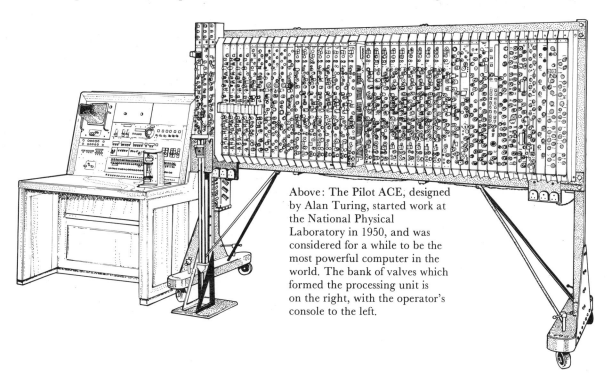

Above: The Pilot ACE, designed by Alan Turing, started work at the National Physical Laboratory in 1950, and was considered for a while to be the most powerful computer in the world. The bank of valves which formed the processing unit is on the right, with the operator's console to the left.

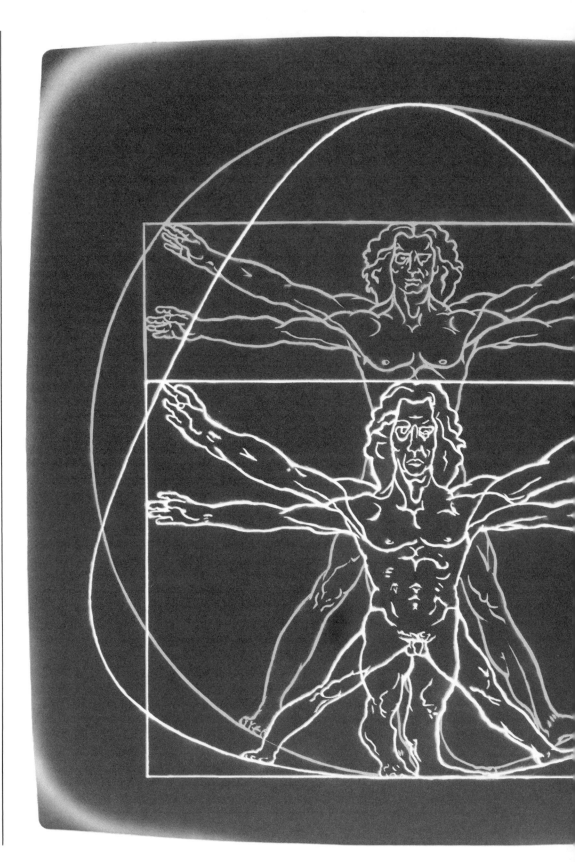

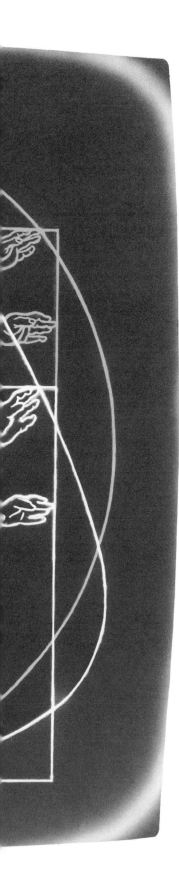

The Revolution Begins

By the half-way point in the twentieth century, computers had proved their worth as extremely fast calculators, capable of tackling a range of tasks which widened with the knowledge and skills of their programmers. Commercial interests were by then taking the plunge and what impressed most users and potential customers was the extraordinary speed with which the devices could calculate. A firm using a properly programmed computer could polish off in less than a week what would have taken an army of humans using hand calculators two or three years. On the other hand, computers were very expensive—you would be lucky to have any change from a million pounds by the time you had installed a decent sized one. They were also large, costly to maintain and inclined to break down at inconvenient moments. Despite all this, when you totted up the pros and measured them against the cons, computers were far better than the humans they were beginning to elbow aside.

This business of speed is particularly important. Babbage's Analytical Engine might have managed a calculation a second—much faster than a human can do and, of course, it was capable of keeping it up all day. Later, electrically driven machines of the Burroughs kind could do several calculations a second, while even the earliest true computers—such as the Harvard Mark I—could cope with dozens. The limiting factor was the speed with which the counting units or switching elements within the device could change their state, and with any mechanical or even electro-mechanical device an upper limit was soon reached. With electronic valves or tubes there was an immediate quantum change. Now there were no moving parts, and the switching activity was the equivalent of an electrical current being turned on or off, which, electricity being what it is, can be done very rapidly. Thus the very first computers using electronic components immediately bumped switching speeds up from dozens to thousands of cycles per second.

So great was the advance that many people working with computers took the complacent line that not only was the upper practical limit of computation speeds near to being reached, but also the upper *required* limit. In other words, the things could now work so quickly that there seemed to be very little point in forcing them along any faster. Better, it was argued, to increase the reliability of valves and do something to reduce their size, their voracious appetite for

Above: The UNIVAC I, brainchild of ENIAC inventors Eckert and Mauchly, was the first commercially successful computer system. More than 50 sales followed the initial delivery to the US Bureau of Census in March 1951. The UNIVAC contained a number of innovations, notably the use of magnetic tape for input. The tape decks can be seen to the right, with the processing unit at the back, behind the operator's console and console typewriter.

power and the huge amount of heat they exuded. Some useful improvements were made along these lines, but it is a feature of a valve that the amount of energy it uses up is almost ludicrously out of proportion to what it delivers at the end. It has been said that it is equivalent to using a complete freight train to haul a single pound of butter.

The inefficiency of valves had been fully recognized long before anyone contemplated making computers with them, and firms which were big in the communications business had for years been sinking substantial research money into discovering an alternative switching amplifier. Working notably hard in this field was the Bell Telephone Company, and in the late 1940s, after twenty years' research, three of their scientists, Bardeen, Brattain and Shockley, well and truly delivered the goods by coming up with the transistor.

If one were to attempt to identify the most important single invention within the whole complex of inventions which we today call the computer, it would undoubtedly be the transistor. Electronic valves made the first high-speed processing possible, and the stored program led the way to the possibility of computer intelligence, but the transistor outranks them all. To appreciate its significance we need to dive once again into detail.

Valves or tubes, as we have said, rely for their amplifying power on a heater electrode which pumps electrons through a vacuum. This electrode is a device which has to be shaped and manufactured out of metal, and it becomes inoperative if it is reduced beyond a certain size. In any case, if it gets too small it cannot produce enough heat to activate the electrons. The transistor, in contrast, does without these metal grids and relies for its actions on particular structures of a minute size which form inside silicon crystals, and these can act as very powerful electronic amplifiers. Thus one can have a "solid state" amplifier based on a tiny fragment of silicon and a very substantial reduction in the size of the functioning unit of a computer becomes possible—indeed the very first transistorized devices occupied less than a hundredth of the space of an old-fashioned tube. But there is another bonus. Because they do not rely on heat to drive their electrons along (transistor radios, as everyone knows, need no "warming up" period) they consume far less energy. They are also faster in operation, and much more reliable. With a bump which was heard around the world, the electronic valve hit the scrap-heap.

The coming of the transistor could not have been foreseen by any of the computer pioneers, nor could its dramatic consequences have been anticipated. The power and speed of all-transistor computers rose to a point where they were quantitatively different from anything that Babbage could have contemplated, perhaps even comprehended. Computer memories also became larger, moving from the paltry hundred or so "bits" of store in the earliest devices to thousands, hundreds of thousands, millions, tens of millions, eventually billions of words in store.

These memories generally were, and still are, of two types: a fast, rather small store from which information could be pulled out at the rate of millions of words *per second*, and a "slow", more or less limitless store where the information was held in the form of magnetic signals on tapes or rapidly revolving discs. In these "slow" stores the access time—the time taken to pull something out of memory—might stretch over such devastatingly long periods as twenty or thirty seconds. Once these massive memories came into being computers began to take on a new and unexpected role. Instead of just being heavy-duty calculators—number-crunchers to use the trade term— they suddenly became information handlers as well, offering huge and progressively cheaper repositories for the terrifying masses of facts and data which our world is endlessly generating.

Throughout the fifties and into the sixties the scope and power of computers continued to expand. Their numbers

Left: The transistor, which revolutionized the development of computers since it removed the dependence on valves, was invented in 1948 by three American scientists, **John Bardeen (b. 1908), Walter Houser Brattain (b. 1902)** and **William Bradford Shockley (b. 1910)**, who were jointly awarded the Nobel Prize for Physics in 1956. Their discovery was made when all three were on the staff of Bell Laboratories. Bardeen (far left) has since become a notable authority on superconductivity and achieved the unusual distinction of a second Nobel Prize for Physics in 1972. Shockley (centre) has aroused more recently considerable controversy over his proposals concerning genetic engineering and the formation of sperm banks.

doubled, doubled again and continued to double, their memory banks increased stupendously, their brontosaurus-like bulks gave way to lighter, smaller frames, their processing speeds increased astronomically, and their cost began to plummet. This may sound like technology run riot—and that is exactly what it was. Never in history had an aspect of technology made such spectacular advances.

Three major motivating forces powered this technological bandwagon, and the first, as is so often the case, was militaristic. The problems of the military are ideal for tackling by computers. Anyone in a command position in a battle is faced with a huge inflow of information, often arriving in bursts and loaded with muddled messages which stretch the human brain beyond its capabilities. The point was nicely made at an early stage in the history of computing when the great Duke of Wellington, accompanied by his wife, visited Babbage while the latter was labouring over the design of his Analytical Engine. Asked if the principal problem of the machine lay in turning up the individual components, Babbage replied that it was more a matter of the inventor grasping the overall complexity of the system, and trying to hold in his mind the infinite variety of consequences that could arise from the interaction of its parts. The Duke, who had faced exactly the same problem when trying to control vast and disorderly assemblies of soldiers and weld them into a smoothly operating whole, knew exactly what he was talking about.

Things have got worse rather than better since Waterloo, as the speed and movement of the individuals and groups in a battle have increased, and it is not surprising that by the late fifties the military powers of the world had become highly interested in harnessing the power of computers to their own ends. The first fruits of this were largely defensive: the SAGE air defence system in the USA, for example, monitored information fed into it, manually and automatically, by tens of thousands of radio and visual observation posts across the North American continent and its oceans, and by integrating this vast array kept the overall defence forces in the appropriate state of readiness. Later, computer systems were called into play to draw up attack strategies; later yet, they found themselves, greatly reduced in size, riding along in strike aircraft, submarines and tanks, and, when miniaturization had really made some headway, in the front end of weapons themselves. All this had its beneficial aspects. In the first place, the sums of money that the United States Government can pull together when it wants to coursed through the world of computers, creating and moulding a subsidiary industry. Secondly, the stringent requirements of the military—who demanded systems that not only worked but also worked reliably under battle conditions—tended to generate tried and tested products which could later be repackaged for the non-military market. In the third place, a huge thrust was given to miniaturization.

The second big motivating force was the Space Race. Just over two decades ago, in 1957, the Russians shocked the world by successfully launching a series of artificial satellites, one containing a dog, while the Americans, who had a nonchalant belief in their own technological superiority, endured a series of toe-curling fiascos in which rockets either blew up on the pad, or rose grandly a couple of hundred feet into the air and fell with a splash in the sea. It was clear that the Russians had moved rapidly ahead in developing big booster rockets, and indeed they remained ahead in the Space Race until about the mid-sixties. The American response to this was partly glorious and partly megalomaniacal, and involved siphoning colossal sums of money into the goal of landing a man on the moon—if possible ahead of the Russians, and in any case before the dawn of the seventies. The outcome of this is well known, and important inasmuch as it showed just what human beings can do if they really put their minds (and their money) to it. But the Space Race also led to an advance in computer science, predominantly because of the tremendous computer back-up which each extra-terrestrial mission required, but partly because of the real need of the Americans to miniaturize until they too had developed their own big boosters. Interestingly enough, the Soviet Union's giant rockets have probably ended up doing them a real disservice by teaching them profligacy. Such movies and TV transmissions as come from Russian spaceships show them to be cavernous things whose interiors are kitted out more like submarines than spaceships and are chock-a-block with chunky equipment, including very chunky computers. The Americans, on the other hand, had to squeeze their technology, computers and all, down to size, and by doing so pushed themselves a decade ahead in miniaturization.

The third great force rolling computers into action was another of Man's most basic (some would say base) motives—commercialism. When people who live in those parts of the world that exist under the banner of capitalism see a chance of making money out of something, they will find a way of doing it. And when they see a way of making a lot of money, they become enormously well motivated to do it. At the very beginning it wasn't clear to even the most far-sighted business entrepreneur that computers were hovering on the edge of being very big business. Indeed the general consensus among both the commercial and the

Burrhus Frederic Skinner (b. 1904), American experimental psychologist influenced by Pavlov and Russell, invented the Skinner Box for training animals to learn appropriate responses. He realized that by division of the learning processes into small parts, pigeons, for example, could be taught quite complex behaviour. Skinner succeeded in teaching pigeons to bowl balls down a toy skittle alley and in teaching them to play table tennis. His work with animal learning and subsequently with teaching machines is recognized as revolutionary for educational method. Skinner was Professor of Psychology at Indiana University from 1945 to 1948; he then became Professor of Psychology at Harvard, and published a number of works on behaviour as well as a novel, *Walden Two*, about life in a Utopian community based on his principles of social engineering.

scientific fraternity was that the world market for computers would be quite a meagre one. One British pioneer,
for example, thought that the entire computer needs of the
UK could be served easily by one big system—and big
system in those days meant the kind of thing that will sit
on the top of a desk by today's standards. Particularly
indicative of how non-obvious was the growth potential of
computers is the fact that hardly any of the many companies
who were doing well manufacturing and selling desk
calculators in the 1940s diversified into computers.

And so, aided by spin-off from military and space
research, and feeding on the growing need for their existence, computers became one of the capitalist world's
major growth industries. To begin with their presence
was barely felt as only large organizations and government
authorities were able to afford to buy them. Then, on the
back of the transistor and with prices sliding fast, small
computers designed for small businesses came into being.
Companies manufacturing computers became highly pro-
fitable and ploughed their profits back into further investment, thus yielding further technological advance and
further profits. As larger-capacity memories were crammed
into ever-smaller spaces and steadily greater reliability
was achieved, brand new applications began to arise.
Machine-readable script appeared on the bottom of
cheques and the banking industry was swept into the world
of automatic data-processing. Airline and chain-hotel
bookings switched over to computers, and after the mid-
1960s no large commercial organization in its right mind
would consider any other way of coping with its salaries
and wages than by computer.

The result was that at about the time that Neil Armstrong
achieved the goal of plonking an American boot on the
moon, computers had reached a point where their infiltra-
tion into large businesses and government departments was
considerable. Three substantial barriers, however, still
stood in the way of their expansion into the world of the
average man, and it was not obvious how those barriers
could be overcome other than by the slow, steady erosion of
time and gently advancing technology. But computers
themselves contain the seeds of their own growth and
technological advance, and the rules which govern the
pace of normal scientific and industrial development do
not always apply. The three barriers blocking their widespread advance were: size, cost and language.

The problem of size needs little debate. In the 1960s
powerful computers were extremely big, and you had to
have large premises—a disused aircraft hangar preferably
—to accommodate them. There were additional problems

in keeping them at an even temperature and in purified air, in supplying them with adequate power and twenty-four-hour-a-day maintenance—the computers of the time didn't like to be switched off and suffered ghastly bouts of total amnesia if they were.

The problem of cost is an even more obvious one, and there is a subsidiary problem which itself handicapped development. If you are the head of a giant corporation which has just parted with a million or so to install a computer, you are going to do all you can to get value for money from it. And that means that you must make sure that it works away doing routine data-processing for as many hours of the day as it can manage. There is going to be no question of allowing any one individual to monopolize it, writing his own software—the generic name for sets of programs—and sitting at a terminal for hours on end with the entire computer at his beck and call. But by restricting usage in this way you ensure that computers remain tied to their number-crunching role, which in turn restricts their chances of moving out into the "real world".

The third problem is that computers spoke in a language of their own—an apparently incomprehensible string of numbers and holes punched on cards or paper tape, none of which made any sense to anyone who hadn't been taught

Above: The increasing demands made upon computer scientists as a result of the development of satellites and rockets provided an intense stimulus to the computer industry. The space-ship Vostok, shown here at the Soviet pavilion at Expo-67, Montreal, contains a number of computers.

the mysteries of machine-language. A new species of being, the programmer, came into existence to cope with these communication problems, and before long they became the indispensable links between normal mortals and the computer they served.

The solution was a fairly obvious one: design a language which any ordinary human could use, and make it at the same time comprehensible to the computer. The task was not too difficult. Remember that in its deepest guts all the computer is doing is juggling millions of switching units whose states are constantly changing from on to off, and that these represent calculations using the binary code. If one arranges for a program to convert the letters of the alphabet into binary number equivalents, the data can be entered in the form of letters—which, in turn, can make up English (or any other language) words and phrases. Further software development of a much more complicated kind is necessary to ensure that the computer understands what to make of some of these words and phrases. Even today the average computer has only a limited repertoire of linguistic understanding, and its knowledge is confined to such useful phrases as RUN, GO, LIST, STOP and so on. Nevertheless the development of these human-type languages greatly simplified the man-computer interface.

The next crucial development came when computer designers realized that any individual sitting at a console and pounding away at the computer was making only the most inefficient use of its time. Here was this horribly slow human solemnly typing in his few commands, which the computer would execute in a microsecond, after which it would have to sit and wait for his next instructions—and during this time it could have solved another million problems had it been given the chance. Something had to be done about this terrible waste, and the solution adopted was known as time-sharing. Using this technique, the computer is provided with a number of access points—"ports" they are called—which allow more than one individual to operate it at any one time. There can be hundreds or even thousands of potential users on really big systems. The computer first looks at the task that user "A" has set, deals with it in the minute amount of time that it needs and instructs the terminal "A" is working on to begin typing out its response. It then moves on to look at user "B", deals with him, moves on to user "C", and so on round the loop.

By the mid-sixties, the processing speeds of big computers had already reached the point where the system's gallop round its ring of users was so fast that it would be back to user "A", waiting like a genie for him to type in his next command, while he was still laboriously reading its previous message. The point is that a few seconds may seem very short to us, but they are absolute aeons to a computer.

This description of time-sharing may have given you a picture of a whole lot of humans sitting pressed up against the side of a large computer, jostling for elbow room to use its terminals. In fact, most terminals were located conveniently on the end of long cables at places where people might want to use them. And once the notion of communicating with the system on the end of a cable was accepted, it wasn't difficult to conceive of the idea of communicating via the telephone network. You simply needed a decoder, which hooked up your terminal to a telephone and converted the signals into a form suitable for phone lines, and a reconverter at the other end where the computer received the unscrambled messages. It was no longer necessary to buy a computer, to find the money to maintain it and a basement to squeeze it into. Somebody else would look after these problems and merely send you a bill for services every month.

For the really big users who had found it essential to invest in computers in the early days, time-sharing and its commercial exploitation offered very little that was new. But for others—such as small businesses, schools, hospitals, even private individuals who would have liked to experiment with computer usage but who could never have even contemplated finding the money to buy one—the development was a godsend. And indeed the late sixties and early seventies saw a sudden explosion of interest by just the kind of users we are talking about—the first transfer of computer power into public hands.

But there was really far more to it than that. Access to computers over telephone lines meant not only human access. Computers, too, could be linked to each other, thus greatly extending their range and power. International barriers began to look oddly thin for the first time, as computers flashed their messages to each other across the Atlantic while their creators still fumbled with baggage in airports. At a big computer conference I organized in 1970, the pièce de résistance on the last day was an experimental hook-up from the conference stage in London to the MIT computer in Boston—a demonstration which was greeted with a murmur of amazement from the by no means unsophisticated audience. On the next day, while eating a plastic lunch on the flight to Boston, I told myself that instead of enduring the terrible boredom of a transatlantic flight, I could easily have done all my business with MIT via the computer. Little did I realize that we would shortly be moving into just that kind of world.

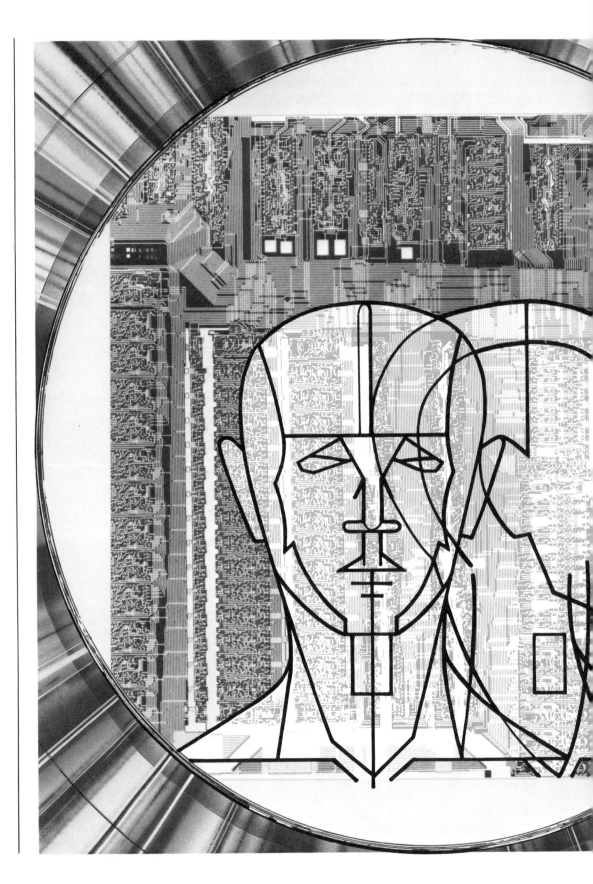

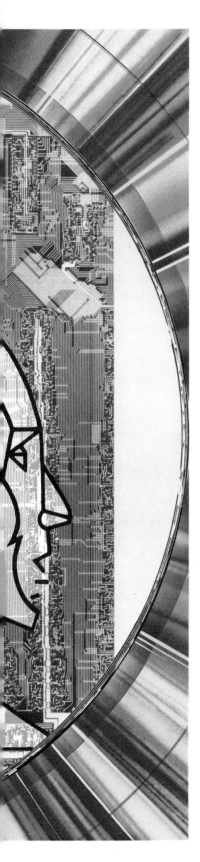

Under the Microscope

This chapter is about very big numbers. That doesn't mean the number of minicomputers used in the canned food industry last year, or the expected growth in the profits of IBM in the period 1980–81, or the total number of cheques processed automatically by the big five British banks. These are big numbers all right, but they have only secondary significance for computers. The numbers I shall be talking about are very large indeed, but they relate to very small things—minute dimensions of space and time.

The first dimension to concentrate on is the spatial one. The components of the earliest computers were large and mechanical. Then came electro-magnetic relays, which were a little smaller, after which came valves which, if anything, were a shade larger. The arrival of the transistor, on the other hand, produced a quite sensational reduction in size. The transistor itself is really a slice of semi-conducting material (a material which is not such a good conductor as metal, but better than, say, wood), which, when it contains certain impurities in its structure, can act as an amplifier and a "solid-state" switching device. It is a curious fact that these impurities can be very small indeed, and yet the transistors still retain their amplifying power. And no sooner had the first transistors been manufactured than scientists were looking at ways of miniaturizing them from their initial size of about one cubic centimetre to something more like a pinhead.

These levels of miniaturization were fairly quickly achieved with the consequence that constructing a computer with ENIAC's nineteen thousand components, but using tiny transistors instead of the original valves, would have brought it down from house size to something more like that of a small room. And while these developments were filtering through on to the market, the transistor engineers were designing whole "logic units"—*complete electronic circuits*, consisting of between twenty and a hundred components and roughly equivalent, I suppose, to Babbage's demonstration Difference Engine—all connected together on a "chip" of silicon about a centimetre square. These chips, incidentally, are now the heart of just about every electronic counting device from watches to the largest computers. We don't need to discuss their actual manufacture, which is not an easy process, but once a "master chip" has been designed and etched out—various techniques are employed in production, including a kind of chemical "growth" process—they can be mass produced.

Miniaturization did not stop when it came to etching complete circuits on a chip. With the technique known as large-scale integration, first hundreds, then thousands, and even tens of thousands of individual units could be amassed on one slice of semi-conductor. And still the process of miniaturization continued, is continuing, and so far as one can see will continue into the foreseeable future. The units of which computers are made are getting smaller and smaller, shrinking beyond the range of ordinary microscopes into the infinities of the molecular world. So rapid is the rate of progress that advance seems to be following advance on almost a monthly basis. The very latest memories, effectively containing hundreds of thousands of switching units, are being squeezed on to a chip, and are already on the market. On the laboratory bench, and scheduled for volume production imminently, are the first million-unit chips.

Now a million is a peculiar number which gets flung around more and more these days as inflation makes government budgets soar into the stratosphere. It is easy, therefore, to devalue the concept of a million pounds, and at the same time devalue the concept of a machine made up of a million individual components, and yet which would still nestle on a fingernail. To get a rough idea of what we are talking about, suppose that one expanded these tiny units up to the size of the valves in the original ENIAC and laid them side by side on a flat surface so that they were two inches apart from each other, what size would this turn out to be? The answer is that it would be as big as a football field.

But let us look at it another way. When the first big computers attracted the attention of the Press in the early fifties, they were given the not totally misleading name of "electronic brains". The human brain itself is made up of minute electronic switching units—they operate on a binary "all or nothing" principle by the way—called neurones, and there are an awful lot of them—about ten thousand million in all. But even assuming that neurones and electronic switching units are functionally equivalent, it was ridiculous, scientists used to argue, to talk of computers as "brains" and even more ridiculous to imagine them doing brain-like things. Why, if you wanted to build a computer which contained the same number of functional elements as the brain, you would end up with something the size of Central London and drawing more power than the whole of the Underground system.

This daunting example was generally used to silence the brain/computer parallelists in the all-valve days of the early fifties and it makes quaint reading when you come across it today. But by the early sixties, with transistorization, the computer/brain shrank to the size of the Albert Hall, and a ten-kilowatt generator would now keep it ticking over nicely. By the early seventies, with integrated circuits, there had been a further compression: it was down to the size of a London bus, and you could run it off a mains plug. By the mid-seventies it was the size of a TV set, and at the late seventies that of a typewriter. And the incredible shrinking brain will continue to shrink—to what size? My guess is that soon it will be no bigger than a human brain, perhaps even smaller. And to power it, a portable radio battery will suffice.

These careering changes, which will shortly lead to computers paralleling the brain both in the size and number of their individual components, do not allow one to draw other parallels. Assuming one makes such a brain model and it sits there, capable of calculating at computer-like speeds, it will still be unable to perform any of the functions of a human brain. To do so it would have to be programmed appropriately, and the programming problems would be colossal. On the other hand this does not imply that it could *never* be so programmed. It is also fair to say that there would be ways in which the natural brain and the brain-sized computer would differ, other than in their software. The computer, for example would have an enormous edge on switching speed. The human brain would be chugging along at a hundred cycles per second, while no computer would be satisfied with a switching speed less than a million cycles! Here again we have to pause and contemplate just what we are talking about.

Most people reckon a second to be rather a short period. There is not much you can do with it—blink an eye, speak one short word or read about ten characters of text. The idea that an electro-mechanical relay can flick back and forth twenty times in a single second sets up an image of a blurring, clattering bit of metal, and when you get to valves operating thousands of times a second you move into a scale of time with which you have no touch-points. But what about *millions* of times a second? Are we not in danger of losing contact with the concept altogether? But then this is just the beginning, and if you have not thought much about these things you had better steel yourself for a shock when I tell you that computers already exist whose switching potential is in the nanosecond range—that is *billions* of times in each tick of the clock. Once again we need to at least try to get this in perspective and can perhaps manage it by spreading time out with a broader brush. Since we so frequently hear the word "billion" employed in terms of money (I am talking about the American billion —a thousand million), let us use a context which is both monetary and temporal.

Imagine a billionaire who decides that he is going to hand out a pound note to everyone who comes up to him—just one pound each. A long line forms and the billionaire starts handing out his pounds. He moves quickly and manages to get rid of them at the rate of one every ten seconds, but being just a human he can only keep it up for eight hours a day, five days a week. How long will it take for him to dispose of his billion? Suppose that he has just handed over his last note, how long ago would it have been since he handed over his first one? Ten years? Twenty? Most people, when asked this question, take a jump in the dark and come up with a figure between ten and fifty years in the past. Once in a while someone will give you a date in the nineteenth century. Does that seem plausible or might it be even earlier? Does it seem conceivable, for example, that the billionaire could have started as far back as the Battle of Waterloo? Well, in fact he would have had to start before that. The Great Fire of London? No, he'd have been counting away while Old St Paul's blazed away. The execution of Anne Boleyn? No, he would have been counting then too. Agincourt? No. The Battle of Hastings? No, further still. To cut a long story short, you would have to go back to the year 640 or thereabouts before you would see the billionaire handing over his first pound note. But that is just a taste of the cake. A billion times per second is no longer considered to be anything like the upper limit of computer processing speeds. Some recent observations indicate that on the surfaces of some of the latest semiconductor materials, tiny magnetic elements can be seen switching, admittedly in an uncontrolled way, at rates approaching a *trillion* a second.

Carry the analogy to a trillionaire who wants to get rid of his money and you dive back in time beyond Christ, beyond Rome, beyond Greece, Stonehenge, Egypt and the Pyramids, before architecture, literature and language, and back to the Pliocene Age, when Europe was encrusted with ice and the mammoth and woolly rhinoceros were the kings. There is really no other word for it—such switching speeds are fantastic. And yet they are real: computers can operate at such speed, and Man will find a way of making use of them.

Which brings us to the question of just what possible use

could be found for these extremely fast, extremely small computers and their even faster, even smaller progeny. Surely there must be an upper limit to the speed with which one would *want* to calculate? To take an extreme example, is it really going to help a company whose total tax and wage structure is handled by its own computer in one hour, to have it dealt with by the next generation of machines in one second? Alternatively, supposing that, using current memory technologies, all personnel details could be recorded on a flat magnetic disc the size of a 45rpm record, what possible advantage could there be in storing it all on something the size of a postage stamp? These may seem to be natural questions, as indeed they are, but they are not the most important ones and they miss one or two big points.

Firstly, while massive increases in processing speeds are helpful when it comes to number-crunching—the kind of company/business tasks we were talking about above—they begin to have far more dramatic yield when the power of the computer is directed towards tasks of a non-numerical nature. The distinction between numerical and non-numerical needs to be made with care, but we are talking about tasks where the computer's intellectual potential, its capacity for problem-solving, for fact finding, for logical analysis rather than for purely routine calculation come to the fore. The use of the word "intellectual" in connection with computers is also treading on dangerous ground, but once computers move from routine to analytical and integrative functions, the increases in processing speed will begin to pay off and they will be able to tackle more complex problems.

The second point concerns reductions in size. Why make computers so small that if you drop one on the floor you are in danger of walking off with it stuck to the heel of your shoe? There are three answers to this question and together they sum up one of the most important single factors about the pace of computer development over the next few years. Very small computers have enormous advantages: firstly, because they consume absolutely minute amounts of power; secondly, because they are very cheap; and thirdly, because they are extremely portable and can therefore be put to use in all kinds of different places. Indeed, we are shortly moving into the phase where computers will become almost the cheapest pieces of technology on earth— cheaper than TV sets (they already are), cheaper than portable typewriters, cheaper even than transistor radios. They will also, for exactly the same reasons, become the most common pieces of technology in the world, and the most useful.

What Makes a Micro Tick

by TOM STONIER

At this point Chris Evans's work comes to an end.

Let us review what he outlined for us. During the seventeenth century, European civilization had reached the point where more and more people were manipulating numbers. The need for automatic devices to aid calculations became obvious, and some of the finest minds of the times addressed themselves to the problem: Napier, Pascal, Leibniz. . . .

By the early nineteenth century, there appeared the grandiose schemes of Charles Babbage, correct in theory, but decades, if not a century, ahead of the physical technology required to put the theory into operation. All those wheels and cogs, levers and rods . . . yet, in a few decades, the machine tool industry had advanced sufficiently to allow the development of mechanical adding machines and calculators.

Then came electricity to drive the gears and to lay the groundwork for the electronic revolution. First electromagnetic relays, then electronic valves to speed up the processes a thousandfold . . . by the end of the 1940s the first generation of electronic computers had become well established. Two more technical breakthroughs: first the transistor, then the development of integrated circuits to the point where they could be put on the silicon (making up the transistor) itself. The result—the microprocessor.

It is these last two stages which we want to look at more closely. The development of the transistor is a fascinating story in its own right. In many ways it parallels the computer story. Just as society had grown to rely heavily on numbers during the seventeenth century so that people began to think about mechanical aids, so did society come to rely heavily on electronics during the second quarter of the twentieth century. And just as the US Census Bureau could no longer handle numbers effectively by the 1880s, so could the military no longer be content with fragile, bulky, unreliable, energy-hungry electronic valves by the end of the 1940s.

The theoretical framework for the development of the transistor can be traced back to at least the 1830s, when Michael Faraday observed that the electrical conductivity of silver sulphide increased upon heating while that of metallic conductors decreased. The first functioning solid state device used subsequently for detecting radio signals was constructed by Ferdinand Braun in 1874. Braun, professor of physics at Marburg, also invented the tuned electric circuit. These devices set the stage for the early radio and wireless industry. The solid state semi-conductor was made out of crystals of galena, a mineral of lead sulphide. The "crystal" sets of early radio fame gave way, in due course, to the electronic valves, invented during the first decade of this century.

The electronic valves eclipsed the need for solid state devices. However, basic research carried on, driven by curiosity and the human need to explore the universe. Max Planck's quantum theory in 1900, Einstein's explanation of the photovoltaic effect in 1905, Roentgen's work on luminescence, all engaged the attention of a young physicist in Berlin, R. W. Pohl. By 1933, Pohl knew enough to predict that electronic valves in radios would, some day, be replaced by small crystals in which flows of electrons could be controlled.

Such crystals were shown to work in the Bell Company Laboratories in New Jersey on 23 December, 1947. At that time Bell Laboratories employed 5700 people of whom at least 2000 were specialists. The combination of a maturing basic science (solid state physics) coupled to a massive investment in R and D by Bell created the transistor. Lest we become overawed by the industrial input into this effort, it might be well to remember that similar work at Purdue University was only a matter of months, perhaps even weeks, away from the same finding. Had the researchers there persevered, the three names associated with the invention of the transistor might have been Benzer, Bray and Lark-Horovitz. Instead, the credit goes to Bardeen, Brattain and Shockley—and so it should.

The transistor, then, is a crystal in which small flows of electrons can be controlled to provide signals. A number of materials have been shown to work, but most of the technology of the last couple of decades has centred on crystals of very pure silicon which have been "doped" with small amounts of some other element such as boron or phosphorus to give the crystal just the right electronic properties.

As Pohl had rightly predicted in 1933, small crystals began replacing the electronic valves. The transistor radio helped to initiate the communicative era. If the older generation viewed with distaste the cacophony associated with this device, it was because they could not know the profound cultural changes Western society was about to undergo—changes which, in the long run, will produce a harmonious global village.

But we are digressing from our story. The transistor radio was still made the way radios were always made. You started with a metal chassis and you placed on this chassis (properly insulated) the various electronic components: resistors, capacitors, transformers, etc., including the transistors. You then wired the whole lot together. This was a slow, laborious process. Like calculating lengthy sums with pencil and paper—there ought to be a better way.

Enter the integrated circuit. As Professor Ernest Braun, Head of Aston University's Technology Policy Unit, has pointed out, the integrated circuit was a commercial innovation developed largely by and within industry (in contrast to the transistor, which, except for the very last steps, was developed in university and basic research laboratories). Instead of soldering wires to various components on a metal chassis in order to connect them, you begin with a board made of plastic (or other non-conducting material) on to which you spray a pattern of thin strips of metallic conducting material. This creates a printed circuit board into which you can then insert the components. Around 1960, this principle began to be extended to spraying conducting materials on to parts of silicon wafers themselves. The silicon chip revolution was beginning.

What is a chip? How is it made? A chip is the equivalent of a printed circuit board ingeniously created on a small sliver of silicon (i.e., on a silicon chip). Remember that the printed circuit board for a computer involves mainly electronic "on/off" switches, and is therefore much less complicated than a radio. During the 1960s, the guts (brains?) of a computer, the processor of information, consisting of batteries of such switches, became miniaturized to the point where each switch consisted of a mere microscopic spot on the silicon chip. The information processor had become a microprocessor. The mighty micro had arrived.

How is a microprocessor made? The process begins with growing very pure, large crystals of silicon. Incidentally, silicon is a very common element on this planet; for example, sand is silicon dioxide. Cylinders of such pure silicon are then sawed like a log into thin wafers, as thin as a knife blade and about the size of the palm of an adult hand. These are then treated in a series of steps which result, firstly, in giving the surface and the interior the proper electronic qualities, and then photoetching different patterns on to the wafers. The patterns actually involve several hundred identical copies across the wafer such that each wafer produces hundreds of small, square units. Each unit, only half a millimetre thick, contains tens of thousands of microscopic (and even sub-microscopic) switches and other electronic elements. This is the microprocessor . . . the miracle chip. The latest techniques involve beams of atoms, electrons and X-rays, allowing a million electronic elements to be placed on a single chip . . . a miracle of production, and a miracle of information power.

How can such a tiny bit of matter handle information? Actually, in principle the microprocessor handles information in much the same way as did old ENIAC and later computers—by means of combinations of switches. The

Below: In the foreground are two wafers from the block of quartz crystal in the background. The wafers or slices are used in the production of a micro chip, as described on the opposite page.

A silicon integrated circuit is produced by building on a silicon slice, about 2mm square and 0.2mm thick, layers of chemicals, each layer acting as an electrical microcircuit. The surface of the slice is specially treated so that the silicon atoms either liberate an electron (in a negative or "n" region) or lose one (in a positive or "p" region). The n and p regions in each layer combine to act as transistors (which amplify current), resistors or capacitors (which store it).

1. The slice is exposed to steam to form an oxide film on the surface. 2. The surface is coated with a light-sensitive material (photo-resist). 3. The first mask is positioned and exposed to light to define a pattern on the slice (here simplified as a circle). 4. The areas exposed to light become hardened (these form the ridges). 5. The non-hardened areas are etched away to reveal the silicon surface. 6. The slice is treated with chemicals which diffuse into the silicon (these are the valley areas). 7. The process is repeated, usually using a different mask for each layer. 8. The finished chip comprises

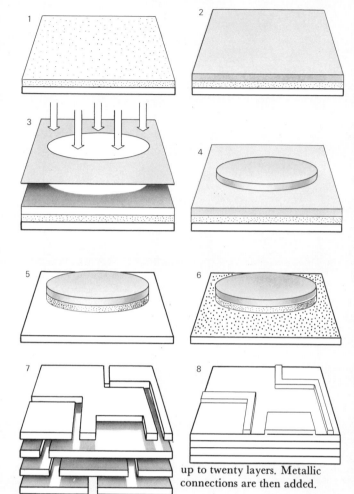

up to twenty layers. Metallic connections are then added.

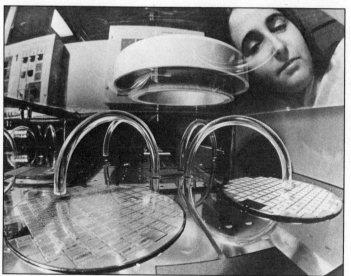

Left: Razor-thin slices of silicon are being processed to become IBM's most advanced memory chips, some of which contain over 65,000 pieces of information. As they move through the air track, clusters of tube-like optical sensor loops detect the presence of the wafers and control their movement through each stage of manufacture.

 Left: The finished chip.

micros just do the job so much faster and much better.

But how can on/off switches handle information? To understand that, we must return to a concept introduced on page 28: binary arithmetic.

Let us begin with the good old-fashioned decimal system we have all become accustomed to. Any quantity can be coded in abstract terms and we have been taught to do so in a decimal system. The decimal system probably reflects the fact that humans have ten fingers. A genius octopus would presumably have invented a numbering system based on eight. A beetle, perhaps, based on six, a millipede on . . . Actually, we do use systems based on something other than ten. Time for instance: $1h:12':42''$ means one hour, twelve minutes and 42 seconds. The system is based on 60, i.e., 60 seconds make the next unit, one minute. In turn, 60 minutes make the next unit, one hour.

The units are arbitrary. It is the code which matters. For example, you can code your ten fingers to count up to 99. With a pen, mark the nail of your left thumb as "50", and each of your fingers on the left hand as "10". On your right hand, mark the thumb as "5", and each finger as "1". Now hold up your hands, look at the backs of them, and think of any number up to 99. Starting with the little finger, put up the appropriate fingers (and thumbs). Try the numbers 12, 22, 39. You can add and subtract as well, but you must be disciplined. (Try 22 plus 12. Then add 39.)

You can also convert the position of your fingers into a binary code using ten fixed places. For example, the number "73" on the Chisanbop technique (that's what it is called) is: left little finger up, left ring finger up, left middle finger down, left index finger down, left thumb up. Right thumb and index finger down, the other three fingers up.

Suppose, now, you write this down on paper by symbolizing a finger up as "1" and a finger down as "0". Using that convention, the number "73" on your fingers reads as: 1100100111. Similarly, ten switches as on (1), or off (0), can symbolize the numbers 1 to 99 in this system. Actually this is a rather inefficient system. Ten switches in the binary system can count to over a thousand, twenty can count to over a million. Roughly, for every ten switches added, the number-handling capability increases a thousandfold over whatever it was before.

Computers using such switches can not only count but, as you did on your fingers, they can add and subtract. Using Napier's trick of converting numbers to their logarithms (another code), computers can multiply and divide by adding and subtracting logarithms. All with simple switches.

To summarize then, a binary system allows you to state any number in terms of "0" or "1". This can be translated into electronic switches as "off" or "on". Thus computers can handle numbers. But computers can handle words with equal ease.

Just stop to think of the way telegrams used to be sent in the old days. It was by telegraph (later radio), using the Morse code. The Morse code used combinations of dots and dashes for each letter—which is, of course, a binary code for letters. A computer can handle such information a million times faster than a telegraph operator by means of micro-electronic switches going on and off. Furthermore, there is no problem in coding not only for letters of the alphabet but also for punctuation marks, special symbols, whole words and phrases. Various combinations of on and off switches can code for these just as easily as if they were numbers.

There is very little information in our heads which cannot be stored as words or numbers. However, the computer can also manipulate information (not only numbers). Here we need advanced concepts, ranging from Boolean algebra and formal logic to information theory. However, take a simple case. It is possible to state propositions and ask questions to which the answer is either true or false, which is, of course, a binary evaluation of statements. "True" or "false" can be recorded by a single switch as "on" or "off".

Two switches could handle "yes", "no", or "maybe". Both switches on means yes. Both switches off means no. One switch on while the other is off means maybe. Other systems can be devised and that's exactly what has been going on—thousands of human brains tinkering with the structure of knowledge to convert systems of human logic into systems of coded electronic impulses.

Tragically, Chris Evans could not develop his vision of the future as he had intended in this book. Fortunately, he gave us much of it in his other books and television series *The Mighty Micro*. He was one of the few who understood fully how fast the future is rushing upon us . . . who made it his mission to prepare us for it.

Undoubtedly, Chris would have been pleased to know that the manuscript for this chapter was typed on a word processor. The pictures in the last chapter are meant to convey the rapid progress made during the past decade in the spread and application of the microprocessors.

Chris lived to see science fiction rocket into reality, then saw that fiction surpassed by the reality of the computer revolution. In reviewing Alexander Korda's movie version of H. G. Wells's *Things to Come*, he points to the moral of that film: ". . . once Man has taken the first step down the path of knowledge and understanding, he must take all those that follow. The alternative is to do nothing, to live with the insects in the dust. . . ."

Amen.

You and the Micro Chip

Setting type for books, magazines, newspapers can all be done on computerized typesetting machines (bottom right). The actual typesetting (keying) is a little faster, but the word output is many times faster. A Monotype machine (bottom left) would take one hour to key 1200 words and the same to produce the type. One computerized setting machine, the Linotron 606, however, would require an hour for the keying of 1500 words and would produce type at the rate of about one million words per hour.

Far right: This solar power calculator works in any good light. It represents a development of silicon technology which allows the silicon to trap sunlight to produce electricity. The two techniques are combined in the device in that the chip is made of silicon and so are the photo-voltaic cells.

Below: This is an educational toy for 4 to 7-year-olds. The machine displays the number 242, for example, and the child with reference to the picture should spell out "beaver". The machine proceeds to the next number if the child gives the correct spelling. The device acts as an introduction to the workings of a computer as well as being an educational game.

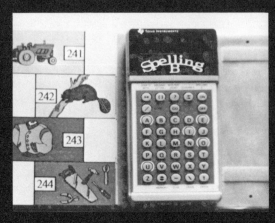

SOLAR POWER
CALCULATOR

Below: Chris Evans operates the Moonlander. This is an advanced training device which can simulate a lunar module landing. It is also used for solving problems, assessing risks and performing complex calculations in space travel. The Moonlander is used as a toy as well.

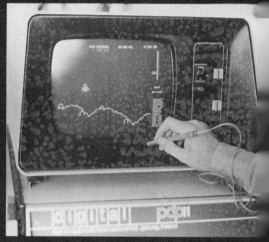

Index

Bibliography

Books
ASIMOV, Isaac (Ed) *Biographical Encyclopedia of Science and Technology* (Pan Books, London 1974)
BODEN, Margaret A. *Artificial Intelligence and Natural Man* (Harvester Press, Brighton 1977)
BOWDEN, B. V. (Ed) *Faster than Thought* (Pitman Publishing, London 1971)
CROWTHER, J. G. *Discoveries and Inventions of the Twentieth Century* (Routledge and Kegan Paul Ltd, London 1966)
DODD, K. N. *Your Book of Computers* (Faber, London 1969)
EAMES, Charles & EAMES, Ray *Computer Perspective* (Harvard University Press, London 1973)
ELWIN, Malcolm *Lord Byron's Family: Annabella, Ada and Augusta, 1816–24* (John Murray, London 1975)
ENTICKNAP, N. (Ed) *Philip's Guide to the Electronic Office* (Input Two-Nine, London 1979)
FOY, Nancy *The IBM World* (Eyre Methuen, London 1975)
GOLDSTINE, H. H. *The Computer from Pascal to Von Neumann* (Princeton University Press, Princeton New Jersey, 1972)
HOLLINGDALE, Stuart & TOOTILL, G. C. *Electronic Computers* (Penguin Books, Harmondsworth 1970)
MARTIN, James *The Wired Society* (Prentice Hall, New York 1978)
MICHIE, Donald *Machine Intelligence* (Edinburgh University Press, Edinburgh 1972)
RALSTON, A. & MEEK, C. (Eds) *Encyclopedia of Computer Science* (Petrocelli, New York 1976)
RANDELL, B. (Ed) *The Origins of Digital Computers: Selected Papers* (Springer-Verlag, New York 1975)
RAPHAEL, Bertram *Thinking Computer: Mind Inside Matter* (W. H. Freeman, Oxford 1976)
RODGERS, William *Think. A biography of the Watsons and IBM* (Stein & Day, New York 1969)
ROSENBERG, Jerry M. *Computer Prophets* (Macmillan, New York 1969)
WEIZENBAUM, Joseph *Computer Power and Human Reason: From Judgement to Calculation* (W. H. Freeman, Oxford 1977)
WINOGRAD, Terry *Understanding Natural Language: A Computer Programme* (Edinburgh University Press, Edinburgh 1972)

Research paper
TURING, Alan M. "Computing Machinery and Intelligence" in *Mind* Vol 59, pp 433–60 (Basil Blackwell Ltd, Oxford 1950)

Periodicals
BYTE (Byte Publications Inc., Peterborough, New Hampshire)
COMPUTER WEEKLY (I.P.C., Electrical-Electronic Press, London)
COMPUTING EUROPE (Haymarket Publishing Ltd, London)
PERSONAL COMPUTING (Benwill Publishing Corporation, Boston)

Tapes
Pioneers of Computing (Science Museum, London) 60-minute recordings of interviews by Dr Christopher Evans with:
1 D. W. Davies
2 Konrad Zuse
3 J. Presper Eckert
4 Jay Forrester
5 Tom Kilburn
6 John Pinkerton
7 Sir Frederic Williams
8 John Mauchly
9 A. D. Booth
10 Jim Wilkinson
Tapes 11 to 20, which are in production, feature:
A. W. Burks, T. H. Flowers, A. W. M. Coombs, R. Slutz, H. H. Goldstine, S. Ulam, H. D. Huskey, C. C. Hurd, M. V. Wilkes, M. Woodger.
Further tapes will include interviews with Grace Hopper, D. Michie, I. J. Good, M. H. A. Newman, J. V. Atanasoff.

Acknowledgements

We are grateful to the following for permission to reproduce the illustrations on pages:
14 Crown Copyright photo Science Museum, London; Mansell Collection; 16 (top) photo Science Museum, London; 17 Popperfoto; 20 photo Science Museum, London; 21 (top and bottom right) photo Science Museum, London; 24, 25 Mansell Collection; 26, 30, 31, 41, 42, 43, 45, 48 photo Science Museum, London; 50 Bettmann Archive; 52 (top and bottom left) IBM; 52 (right) Burroughs Corporation, Michigan; 55 photo Science Museum, London; 58 Crown Copyright photo Science Museum, London; 59 MIT Historical Collection; 62 Popperfoto; 63 Courtesy of Bell Laboratories; 69 Professor Konrad Zuse; 74–75 Harvard University, Cruft Photo Laboratory; 78 Crown Copyright PRO (By Permission); 79 National Physical Laboratory; 84 (top and centre) Sperry Univac; 84 (bottom) Moore School of Electrical Engineering, Pennsylvania; 87 Professor Wilkes, Cambridge Computer Laboratory; 88 Dept. of Computer Science, University of Manchester; 89 Professor Wilkes, Cambridge Computer Laboratory; 92 Sperry Univac; 94–95 Courtesy of Bell Laboratories; 99 Novosti Press Agency; 102 Ferranti/Science Photo Library; 110 Professor Tom Stonier; 111 IBM; 114, 115 Professor Tom Stonier.

Editor
Anne Charlish
Art Director
Nicholas Eddison
Picture research
Anne-Marie Ehrlich
Production Manager
Kenneth Cowan
Production Editor
Fred Gill
Research consultant
Nicholas Enticknap
Illustrators
Hugh Dixon (pages 26/27, 38/39, 52/53, 60/61)
Andrew Farmer (pages 14/15, 32/33, 46/47, 64/65, 80/81, 90/91, 102/103)
David Parr/Studio Briggs (pages 16, 17, 22, 23, 24, 30, 44, 49, 51, 54, 89, 111)